Teaching Canada for the '80s

A. B. Hodgetts
Paul Gallagher

Curriculum Series / 35
The Ontario Institute for Studies in Education

THE ONTARIO INSTITUTE FOR STUDIES IN EDUCATION has three prime functions: to conduct programs of graduate study in education, to undertake research in education, and to assist in the implementation of the findings of educational studies. The Institute is a college chartered by an Act of the Ontario Legislature in 1965. It is affiliated with the University of Toronto for graduate studies purposes.

The publications program of the Institute has been established to make available information and materials arising from studies in education, to foster the spirit of critical inquiry, and to provide a forum for the exchange of ideas about education. The opinions expressed should be viewed as those of the contributors.

© The Ontario Institute for Studies in Education 1978
252 Bloor Street West, Toronto, Ontario M5S 1V6

ISBN 0-7744-0167-2   Printed in Canada
Cover design: Fred Huffman

1 2 3 4 5 MD 28 18 08 97 87

Contents

Preface

It is undeniable that significant improvements in studies of Canada have taken place over the past ten years. Any analysis of progress, however, does not inspire confidence that a generation of truly well-informed young Canadians, sensitive to the interests and concerns of their fellow Canadians or of Canadian society as a whole, is near at hand. Small and active groups of teachers will continue to devote their own time to the development of new teaching materials or to the discussion of new approaches to teaching. A commercial publisher will develop a few outstanding books that students will find challenging and inspiring. A school board here and a teachers' association there will decide that something serious in the field of Canadian studies must become one of their priorities. Three or four faculties of education will somehow find the energy to reform their social studies education curriculum to recognize that their graduates are most likely to teach Canadian children in a school in Canada – and that Canadian schools and Canadian children are not necessarily identical to their counterparts in other societies. Even a few Departments of Education will go beyond hiring specialists to prepare curriculum "guidelines" for distribution to teachers by providing funds to make it possible for teachers to retrain and implement those guidelines. An enterprising university will muster the determination to do what they have been urged to do for years – to cross traditional departmental and faculty barriers and provide for some Canadians a solid academic and professional preparation for a teaching career. Some organizations and privately funded bodies will actually make the effort to find out what others are doing and will devise a way of sharing their resources in their mutual interest. Some leaders in Canadian education will recognize that jurisdictional boundaries are not obstacles to cooperation, that what is happening in Canadian society is relevant to what Canadian schools ought to be doing right now, that education is less tidy but more important than administrative simplicity, and that educational risk-taking is what leadership is all about.

And Canadians care. Certainly many Québecois care enough about their children to say loudly and clearly that Canada as it has been constituted is not for them. It is obvious they plan to use their schools to ensure that the next generation of Québecois will stand with dignity beside or apart from their Canadian colleagues. Albertans care enough to chart as far as they can their own economic future without deference to the Ontario establishment. Atlantic Canadians care enough to insist on jobs, not handouts, from Ottawa and to initiate a real revival of Atlantic culture. Ontarians care enough to have applied sufficient political pressure to force a reform of the school system in general and of Canadian studies in particular.

Canadians care enough to express their frustration about their schools time and time again. They know – or they sense – that something is dramatically wrong, but they are unable to identify the wrong and therefore unable to apply the pressure to it. While some Canadians have simply abandoned any real hope of improvement, most look to Canadian educators for the leadership to diagnose, to propose, and to implement real change. So far, few Canadian educators have provided that leadership.

A plateau in the development of Canadian studies has been reached. Gains of recent years will cause some ripples and touch more teachers and students. However, without any major new departure, a new level of achievement is unlikely. The need now is for something more than merely continuing or expanding what is already being done. The need is to go beyond the broadening of the consciousness of Canadian teachers, beyond developments in teacher education, beyond encouraging teachers to work together across linguistic, cultural, and geographic barriers, beyond the design and development of new books and materials.

The need now is for a cooperative and systematic nation-wide effort to improve the quality of studies of Canada in Canadian schools. The development of a common framework for studies of Canada – but not a consensus story of Canada – is a practical proposal.

A common framework of studies, consistently "pan"-Canadian in objective and designed in truly "pan"-Canadian fashion, touching all curriculum areas and spanning the full range of school years in a coordinated manner, is now the pressing need. Cultural and regional solitudes, in Canadian education as in Canadian society, must work with one another in the common interest. Students throughout Canada, and Canadian society, have every reason to expect the leadership required to develop a distinctively Canadian civic education. This is the real challenge of the '80s to Canadian educators.

A. B. Hodgetts
Paul Gallagher

vi

Acknowledgments

Teachers from every province and from every level of Canadian education contributed to this book. Far too numerous to single out, the participants in the work of the Canada Studies Foundation provided the experience on which the main arguments of this book are based.

An initial draft and outline were reviewed by Stephen Clarkson, John Meisel, Pierre Savard, J. E. Hodgetts, and A. M. Campbell. Their scholarly observations and criticisms were invaluable.

A series of preliminary working papers were submitted to more than one hundred Canadian educators and scholars for comment. Persons deeply involved in the work of the Foundation, and others quite unfamiliar with the Foundation but vitally concerned about the education of young people in Canada, provided most practical suggestions and reactions. The curriculum directors in two provinces provided especially perceptive comments, and all members of the Foundation Secretariat during 1975–78 played integral roles in the drafting and redrafting stages. R. M. Anderson and John S. Church were particularly helpful.

Two people virtually played the role of co-authors. Benoît Robert worked side by side with us at all stages and will be instrumental in the development of a French-language version of this book. George S. Tomkins was painstaking with his reviews and will extend the messages of this book into professional and pedagogical fields shortly.

We wish to acknowledge the assistance of the Royal Canadian Legion. Through a substantial subsidy to a major project of the Foundation, the Legion indirectly enabled us to complete some of the cross-Canada consultation.

We particularly appreciate the efforts of John Main of OISE Publications Division and Diane Mew, our editor, in helping bring the manuscript to a final state of preparation. Debby Markland and Madeleine Solis-Gwilliam, who kept the authors on course and the paper in order, provided far more assistance than their secretarial tasks would indicate.

We hope this book will sustain and extend exciting Canada Studies work now in progress in many Canadian educational jurisdictions. More modestly, we hope it will be of assistance to those engaged in curriculum planning and in the education of teachers. Above all, we hope it will be of practical value to classroom teachers throughout Canada to whom both of us owe so much.

CHAPTER I

Pan-Canadian Understanding: the Priority

It is now a decade since the National History Project brought out its report entitled *What Culture? What Heritage?* Based on an extensive two-year fact-finding investigation from coast to coast, the report presented a severe indictment of what the schools were teaching our young people about their own country. Studies of Canada in all provinces, for a variety of reasons that were carefully documented, tended to contribute to the divisiveness then evident in Canadian society. The Director of the project drew particular attention to the differing and frequently contradictory interpretations of the Canadian heritage presented to English- and French-Canadian students and wrote that:

The lack of understanding between our two main linguistic communities is in part the direct result of what these young people have been taught in school. . . . Canadian studies in the schools of both linguistic groups do very little to encourage a mutual understanding of their separate attitudes, aspirations and interests. Successive generations of young English- and French-speaking Canadians raised on such conflicting views of our history cannot possibly understand each other or the country in which they live.

The report of the National History Project argued that the shortcomings of Canadian studies took on the dimensions of a national disgrace both for individual students who deserved a more rewarding learning experience and for Canadian society whose future was very much at stake. It called for a nation-wide search for effective ways of using the potential of formal education to create a better-informed and more rational society – an effort whose objective should be "not national unity but national understanding."

The publication of *What Culture? What Heritage?* led directly to the establishment of the Canada Studies Foundation – a privately financed five-year project designed to experiment, using voluntary interprovincial cooperative techniques, with ways to improve the quality of Canadian studies in the elementary and

1

secondary schools of the ten provinces and to provide opportunities for classroom teachers and other educators from different parts of the country to meet and work together across regional, linguistic, and cultural boundaries on questions of mutual concern.

Owing partly to the work of the Foundation and the activities and interests of a great many other organizations and dedicated individual educators, and partly to the general temper of the times, there has been a tremendous surge in Canadian studies in recent years. Teaching methods, learning material, and pre- and in-service teacher training, course prescriptions, and the growth of a network of communications between people interested in Canadian studies have all experienced substantial improvements. It is apparent that many of the findings documented in *What Culture? What Heritage?* are no longer applicable to Canadian education.

Nevertheless, the present Canadian studies movement has tended to emphasize regional, provincial, or ethnic issues and concerns, in-depth historical or micro-sociological investigations of one particular group, area, or activity as well as curriculum models and other strictly pedagogical considerations. No one should dispute the value of this emphasis. Local studies are culturally supportive and enriching. In themselves, however, they are unlikely to encourage the kind of pan-Canadian understandings and respect this country seems to need, and indeed they can inadvertently strengthen regional or ethnocentric prejudices. At least they should be supplemented with studies of Canada consciously designed to broaden the perspectives of young Canadians from the local or regional to the wider national and international scene.

In our work with the CSF, we have found that the normal social process by which our young people develop their values, attitudes, and standards of judgment through strong regional and ethnic forces is not yet balanced in formal education by sufficient opportunities to study, to know about, and to understand Canada as a whole. We believe that *Canada* studies – as distinct from all other more restricted *Canadian* studies – should deal with our society as a totality, in country-wide, interlocking perspectives that can be shared by all Canadians wherever they may live. Otherwise, as the National History Project and many others have emphasized, this area of education will continue to be another divisive force in our society.

The Canadian studies movement, in all its variety of techniques and products, should be sustained and nourished. What is needed now, however, is a common framework of ideas that educators in all provinces should use in the development of Canada Studies that will be country-wide in perspectives and objectives. The traditional Canadian practice of different groups and jurisdictions concurrently and independently searching for answers to specific provincial or regional concerns needs to be supplemented by an interprovincial cooperative attack on problems shared by all groups and jurisdictions. The luxury of each going off in his own direction can no longer be afforded, financially or educationally, in Canada.

This book is exclusively addressed to the question, "What should young Canadians *understand* about their own country?" We have consciously and often reluctantly omitted references to curriculum theory and practice, teaching methods, detailed consideration of scope and sequences, the precise knowledge

2

required to develop the understandings and pedagogical concerns. Questions of this kind are best answered by provincial or local authorities in the light of their own particular needs.

This book describes understandings about the nature of Canadian society, the structure and functioning of its economic and political systems, and the problems or public issues that have been of continuing concern to Canadians. While being concerned, of course, with the learning experiences of students while they are still in school, the main emphasis in the following chapters is on understandings that should help them as citizens to participate constructively in the civic – that is, the public – life of Canada. A program of studies designed for this purpose is "civic education" in the widest and best meaning of the term. Obviously, there should be no confusion between this kind of civic education and the old "civics" courses, which dealt almost exclusively with a description, frequently an unrealistic one, of the structure of the government.

There should be a conscious modesty and some degree of caution in any approach to civic education. One of the effects of science and technology has been to give man a new sense of power to manipulate or engineer individuals and societies. Far from advocating any attempt at social engineering, this book suggests in several places that we may need a new ethic which recognizes the limits of men's power over the non-human environment and over each other. Our approach to civic education is designed to help young people acquire the necessary knowledge, understandings, intellectual skills, and feelings of social competence which may eventually eliminate at least some of the feelings of apathy and alienation apparent in a society whose major institutions seem to be growing more remote and impersonal.

The recommendation that the understandings described in this book should be shared by Canadians wherever they may live must not be misinterpreted. In no way should this be seen as advocating the development of some conforming, monolithic, nationalistic spirit; nor should it be taken as underwriting the present federal system of government or searching for a single Canadian identity. The book's emphasis is on the pluralism and diversity of Canada and the opportunities and difficulties presented to Canadians by our regional, economic, social, cultural, and linguistic differences. A basic premise in the following chapters is that conflict of opinion, controversy, and stress are not only inevitable in all societies but are also, within broad limits, a constructive force leading to human betterment. Another basic premise is that an overemphasis on our differences may obscure the fact that, along with people from all other countries, Canadians together face some gigantic, world-wide problems in which we all have a stake.

For most mortals, understanding is a product of knowledge. The possession of knowledge, of course, is no guarantee of compassion or the humane use of reason. Frequently, it is feelings and emotion that sustain our most cherished beliefs. Yet it is primarily by raising the knowledge levels of our students that we may hope to achieve the kinds of understandings and respect for others that are the attributes of a civilized people.

The suggestion that the schools can make a greater contribution to the quality of life in Canada is made in full awareness of the limits to the power of formal education. These limits are imposed, in part, by the human frailties of students,

3

teachers, and other educators; by the influence, for good or ill, of family, peer group, the mass media, and many other factors external to the classroom; by the strength of feelings and attitudes on which the effects of education must always be somewhat unpredictable; and by the subconscious, irrational elements in human nature. Research in political behavior indicates that the power of formal education to influence the thoughts and actions of individuals in a society is highly uncertain. It has been found that education may weaken or reinforce prejudice; it may foster understanding or intensify distrust; it may encourage interest or apathy and it certainly has not always ensured rational social behavior.

It is possible to use these findings as reasons for indifference toward any new approaches to the study of Canada. Students of political behavior, however, are not denying the possible value of reforms in the school system; they are simply showing that the schools and universities have not yet found ways to use their full potential for improving the quality of civic life. Furthermore, very few social scientists have investigated what actually goes on in the classroom or lecture hall. They have been concerned with the end product, with attitudes, voting patterns, and so on, and not with learning materials or teaching methods, which are such important factors in determining the effects of formal education. Rather than weakening the case for reform, current research supports the need for more appropriate and realistic approaches to the contribution education might make to Canadian society.

Surely the need is obvious and urgent. Climates of opinion in Canada range from blissful acceptance of the affluent, consumer-oriented society and confidence in the power of technology and unlimited human progress, to vague feelings of discontent and insecurity, to serious questioning of present values and life-styles, to dire predictions of man's fate on a limited planet, to the philosophies of despair that find life meaningless and absurd.

Manifestations of social dislocations and dangerously high levels of tension in Canada are readily apparent: immediate problems of high rates of inflation and unemployment; the confrontations between management and labor and between governments; the sheer size, power, and remoteness of many political and economic institutions and the resulting feelings of alienation of many people; the polarization of opinion about the role of governments in economic life; the harshness and divisiveness of party politics; the disputes over continentalism and the control of our economy, rural decay, uncontrolled urban growth, and the gigantic problems of the cities; the persistence of severe regional economic disparities; the controversies between environmentalists and developers; the anger and frustration of native peoples; growing ethnic awareness and ethnic rivalries; the disputes over language rights in several provinces and the continuing lack of any real understanding between the two founding cultures – these are only a few of the many signs of stress and discontent in Canadian society.

Many thoughtful Canadians regard these obvious issues as symptoms of more fundamental trends in society. Increasingly, we hear calls for a reappraisal of our values and attitudes toward life. Society, we are told, has lost its capacity for self-discipline; it no longer responds to traditional restraints; it suffers from an excessive concern for self and a deepening subjectivism. Children are being raised in a moral vacuum; the majority of adults are content with the hedonistic

4

values of the fun culture; and so on. Whatever our own thoughts may be on these views of society, there can be little doubt of the continuing need to reconcile individual freedom with an ordered social existence; to recognize the possible disruption of democracy by internal stress; and to give more intensive consideration to the contribution civic education might make to society.

A new element was inserted into all of our uncertainties when a political party dedicated to the separation of Quebec from the rest of Canada came to power in November 1976. The victory of the Parti Québecois now calls into question all the legal, political, and economic relationships dating back to 1867 that most Canadians until recently have tended to take for granted. What, then, is the value of this book – started well before the Parti Québecois victory and designed to describe understandings that all Canadians should try to acquire – when the future of the country is in doubt?

From its inception long before the PQ victory, the Canada Studies Foundation emphasized in its many position papers, seminars, and the public statements of its officers that Canadian federalism was delicately balanced and could disintegrate through internal stress; also, that federal–provincial relations frequently deteriorated into confrontations and that the only method available to resolve these conflicts was hard-nosed political bargaining, as if the provinces and the federal government were separate countries. At the same time, we emphasized that political and economic problems, however severe they might appear to be, were simply challenges to society, offering opportunities for human betterment provided that Canadians had the capacity to handle their difficulties wisely.

We also took the position that in an ever-changing society with so many future options open to it, the Foundation simply could not support any one alternative in any public issue. The validity of this position was apparent in the educators who worked with the Foundation and who represented Canadian society in microcosm. They came from every province and almost every major ethnic, cultural, and linguistic group; their personal viewpoints reflected virtually all shades of political and economic opinions that can be found in Canada. Thus, the very nature of Canadian society dictated that the Foundation should encourage open, intellectually balanced Canada studies designed to provide opportunities for our young people to acquire the knowledge and understandings to respect the values, viewpoints, and interests of Canadians from other groups and regions.

The present climate of opinion in Canada does present a serious dilemma to educators. Recent events in Quebec, combined with various economic and political discontents in other provinces, have created a crisis atmosphere. Stopgap solutions will be put forward and Canadians will continue to face this uncertainty as long as we fail to use fully the tremendous power of education. But because time is short, because there is a crisis, people falsely assume that it is too late for their schools and universities to play a constructive part.

In a country like ours, the long-term chances for survival in some viable political form depend on the skills, knowledge, and wisdom of Canadians and their abilities to resolve conflicts and controversy with understanding and respect for opposing viewpoints. These qualities can be greatly enhanced – indeed may only be enhanced – by the use in our schools of a set of basic understandings about this country that all Canadians can share. By neglecting the slow process of formal education, a society can fail to provide the enlightened public support, the basic consensus, required to ensure its survival. In a democratic society professing to believe in the value of education, we should no longer continue to make this mistake.

Written almost ten years ago, *What Culture? What Heritage?*, after recommending some ways to improve the quality of Canada studies in the schools, concluded with these words:

All of us would agree that Canada is a vast and wonderful land; in places it is spectacularly beautiful; it has been richly endowed by nature; it has already achieved some greatness. We should count ourselves among the very fortunate few of all the peoples on earth to live here. Possessing almost every advantage, we are capable of building a more rational political community, approximating the democratic ideal. What a tragedy it would be if, through lack of foresight or determination, we squandered this opportunity.

The situation in which we now find ourselves seems to indicate that we have indeed partially squandered this opportunity over the past decade. Despite the tremendous surge in Canadian studies and the experimental efforts of the Canada Studies Foundation and many other groups, we obviously need to redouble our efforts to find more effective ways of helping young Canadians to understand the country in which they live and whose future they will partially determine. We should not allow yet another ten years to pass by. This book is presented to educators and all other interested Canadians in every part of the country as a guide – or at least a starting point – to teaching about Canada in the next decade.

Even at times like this, however, it would be a mistake to be too inward-looking and soul-searching. Many of the most important issues facing Canadians are regional or national manifestations of world-wide problems whose magnitude transcends purely domestic issues. The significance of these issues can be obscured – indeed, we believe that they are being obscured both in schools and society – if Canadians are too preoccupied with internal controversies.

World problems must be resolved in the international political arena by diplomacy. The issues are so dangerous and surcharged with emotion that the political arena could become a cockpit. If diplomacy fails, if reasoned solutions cannot be found, nations will continue to use economic and military power, with nuclear warfare as the final arbitrator. Canada simply cannot compete in power politics. This country has everything to gain and absolutely nothing to lose by attempting to pursue a rational foreign policy. It is most likely to be able to do so if Canadians have a better knowledge and understanding of the issues, if they have wider perspectives and a more sensitive feeling of proportion, and if their leaders are free from excessively divisive domestic concerns. This may be an unwarranted confidence in man's rationality, divorced from the harsh realities of today's world; but for Canadians, indeed for most of humanity, there simply is no choice.

For this reason, we believe Canada Studies should be deeply concerned with such things as population explosions; world food and water shortages; the widening gap between rich and poor nations, between the affluent and consumption-oriented and the poverty-stricken and survival-oriented; the ever-increasing ex-

6

ploitation of non-renewable resources; the degradation of the natural environment; rampant world-wide inflation, and other staggering difficulties facing humanity. This emphasis should help Canadian students to widen their horizons, to raise their perspectives from local, regional, or ethnocentric concerns to national and international levels, to give them more sensitive feelings of proportion and a greater awareness of which problems really are significant, and so enable them to better understand their own society.

If we believe that Canada has meaning, that it is a unique country, that it is an organism greater than its parts, that it has the potential to satisfy the basic needs of all its citizens, and that it should continue as a viable community of one kind or other; if we perceive Canada as a delicately balanced federation under inevitable stress; if we appreciate the need for at least minimum levels of understanding and mutual respect among our citizens; and if we believe that all Canadians have a shared interest in trying to find answers to world-wide problems whose importance exceeds most of our immediate concerns – then surely we should no longer allow the vertically structured educational systems of Canada to prevent us from agreeing on the need for the development of understandings about Canada that should be used in the schools of all provinces.

CHAPTER II

Canada Studies: the Basic Components

A civic education based on the analysis of Canada as a political community offers a unique, wide-ranging, yet reasonably structured approach to Canada Studies. This approach requires a knowledge and understanding of the basic features of the country and how these features have interacted to determine the structure of Canadian society, its many diversities, and the mutual aspirations of its citizens as well as their disagreements. This kind of civic education must also deal with public issues, controversies, and tensions that inevitably arise in Canada as a result of its historic development and diversities. It provides many opportunities to study the nature and causes of tension and to understand its negative and positive dynamic powers in our society. Since a great deal of social stress arises through competition in economic life, a reasonably detailed overview of the structure and functioning of Canada's economic system also must be included. Finally, the study of Canada as a political community requires some knowledge and understanding of the structure and functioning of governments and of political processes that have such a pervasive influence on the lives of all Canadians.

The expression "political community" is simply a convenient, value-free term used here to describe any group of people living within recognized, clearly defined geographic boundaries, having a system of government and other shared institutions, and possibly a minimum set of common goals. A political community is composed of many other communities or interest groups based on such factors as family, neighborhood, region, ethnic origin, religion, language, occupation, and economic status. These interest groups may have very specific goals and frequently receive from their members a deeper personal commitment, a more intensive loyalty, than the less tangible political community ever does. Controversy and tension between the differing viewpoints, positions, desires, and power of these diverse groups are inevitable in any society.

It is the fundamental, persistent diversities in a society that make governments and political activity essential. Politics is the process used when attempting to promote an interest or resolve conflict, and government is the agency through which political activity takes place. In other words, politics is often about disagreements and controversy; when there is general agreement there need be no real political activity. This does not mean that society is always in a turmoil or that consensus is never achieved in politics. The balancing of interests, the resolution of conflict, and the lessening of tension are among the principal purposes of political activity. But the solution to a problem usually generates a new set of conditions and tensions. Public issues are seldom fully and permanently resolved. Even when they are resolved and have disappeared from politics, there will always be others arising from the basic differences between people and groups.

Political activity occurs at all levels of government. At the municipal or provincial level, the controversies may be about issues, frequently very intense ones, that are strictly local or regional. Many others are local manifestations of problems that are national or international in scope. The inevitable diversity of all societies makes political activity a permanent and vitally important condition of life.

Political activity is not confined to governments. There are "politics" within trade unions, office hierarchies, corporate board rooms, and so on. These kinds of politics are not important for society as a whole unless they affect the strategies that any interest group attempts to use in pursuing political goals. Politics within the bureaucracy and other agencies of government are of much greater significance because they may strongly influence the ways in which the political system takes initiatives or responds to the demands made on it.

It can be argued that beneath the surface appearance of conflict, politics is really a process of striving for underlying common social purposes and that the inherent rationality of men and women and their sense of universal humanity make them seek agreement and the common good. This idealistic element undoubtedly exists in society and, at times, can be a powerful force in a political community. However, it would be unrealistic not to recognize that attempts to define common goals, and particularly the means by which they may be achieved, are in themselves frequent causes of disagreement and tension.

More often than not in the history of democratic societies, the only points of agreement appear to be on certain basic principles such as willingness to abide by the rules, to use only legal means to achieve political ends, and to accept compromise solutions. Even so, the persistent use of violence and the denial of fundamental democratic understandings is another condition of life with which all political communities must deal.

Diversities, problems, controversies, tensions, and political activities are not only inevitable in all societies, but are also, within broad limits, desirable. Under favorable circumstances, tension is a dynamic, constructive force. Problem-solving within a political community can be a creative experience, lifting a society to new plateaus of achievement. A political community also requires a minimum ability among its citizens to resolve conflict with tolerance, knowledge, and understanding of opposing viewpoints. Without this ability, the tensions may cease to be beneficial and become debilitating or destructive. The solution to a problem may

10

be postponed too long; attitudes in and interests then have time to harden and the range of alternatives is gradually reduced. Bargaining from fixed positions within a very narrow range of choices invariably increases tension and makes democratic compromise exceedingly difficult. The solution to any problem reached in an atmosphere of high tension and crisis is usually unsatisfactory and temporary. Thus one crisis may breed another more serious one, a process that can continue until the opportunities for choice and compromise disappear entirely. The history of many individual countries and of international relations, as well as the present world scene, provides classic illustrations of this tragic tendency in human affairs.

This study of Canada as a political community should not be interpreted merely to mean that Canadian elementary or secondary school students should have traditional courses in political science or economics – although these are valuable electives for some students in several provinces. The richness of our approach to civic education is in its emphasis on Canadian society as a whole, the basic forces that have helped to shape it, the relationships between the vast diversity of people who live here, and a broad working knowledge of the major political and economic institutions Canadians have devised to satisfy their wants.

Although this approach is obviously oriented toward the social sciences, students and teachers will find ample opportunities through literature and art – indeed it would be sad if they did not do so – to see what the creative imagination of Canada's writers and artists have had to say about their own country. Since the quality of life in any political community ultimately depends on the ways in which its individual citizens think, feel, and behave, there are also numerous opportunities here for studies of human nature, of how this nature is manifested in the Canadian character, and of open-ended, somewhat philosophical questions concerning the qualities this country seems to require in its people.

A clear distinction may now be made between Canadian studies and Canada studies. The adjective "Canadian" describes a much broader field of study, including all kinds of local or specialized concerns, as well as a wide range of human activities of no direct political significance. In the remainder of this book, the terms "Canada Studies" and "civic education" will be used synonymously to mean the study of Canada as a political community. Through civic education students can learn to appreciate the values, viewpoints, and interests of Canadians from other groups and regions; to understand the nature of tension, the issues causing it in Canada, the need for political action and the basic principles under which such action should take place; to become more aware of the complexities and challenges they must face as Canadians. Civic education, as defined here, is specifically designed to encourage a development of the skilled and sensitive public opinion needed to resolve deep-seated differences in the Canadian political community before tension levels become dangerously high.

UNDERSTANDING THE BASIC FEATURES OF CANADA

The Canadian political community has been and continues to be primarily formed and influenced by a number of readily identifiable characteristics or basic features that collectively make Canada a unique country. The most important of these basic features are:

11

1. **Canada is a northern, vast, and regionally divided country.**
2. **Canada has a broad natural resource base composed of both renewable and non-renewable resources.**
3. **Canada is an industrial, technological, and urbanized society.**
4. **Canada is a culturally diverse, multi-ethnic country with two historically predominant linguistic and cultural groups.**
5. **Canada is exposed to a multitude of external economic, political, and cultural influences.**

It is essential to understand that the influences of these basic features seldom if ever operate in isolation. They interact with each other to create a complex set of forces that have profound effects on all aspects of life in Canada. Picking out single strands for study from this closely woven fabric, as we have tended to do, is most unlikely to give students a realistic view of Canada. Studies of "regionalism" or "cultural diversity" or more specific topics such as "labor-management relations" undertaken without due consideration for other interacting forces will not achieve the objectives of civic education in a country like Canada. One of the most important intellectual skills for Canadian students to develop is the ability to think about almost any aspect of public life in terms of the interrelated effects of the five basic features of the country.

The importance of these interrelationships will be demonstrated later. However, a quick illustration may be helpful here. In studying Canada's northern geographic location and its natural resources, it would not be particularly useful for students only to acquire purely descriptive information on the location of coal in Cape Breton, iron ore in Labrador, nickel-copper deposits in the Sudbury district, hydro-electric power in the James Bay area, oil and gas reserves in Alberta and the high Arctic, or lead-zinc deposits in British Columbia.

This kind of student work could be immediately made more significant and interesting by designing questions based on any one of the other basic features of Canada: for instance, the fact that it is a technological and industrialized society. Once students have an initial understanding of what these terms mean, they could consider questions such as: What technological demands on our natural resources in the past have greatly altered the directions of Canada's growth from time to time? What kinds of jobs are thus created and what is the ratio of labor to capital requirements? Which resources are renewable and which are not? What are the rates at which this exploitation is growing? Can the non-renewable resources withstand these pressures? What is the impact of technology and industrialization, not only on the resources themselves but also on the natural and human environment? These are only a few of the many questions that might be used to help students understand the ways in which two of the five basic features interact with each other to produce important consequences for Canadians.

Emphasis on the power of the basic features of Canada to shape our society should not be regarded as economic, geographic, or other forms of determinism. Individuals and groups, of course, have the capacity to redirect some of these forces and to modify their effects on society. Nevertheless, either directly or indirectly, the basic features of Canada provide strong constraints within which policy formation, leadership, and authority must be exercised and public opinion formed in Canada.

The interactions of the five basic features of Canada primarily determine the following aspects of public life in this country:

- most of the significant problems, issues, controversies, and resulting tensions that are of continuing concern to Canada;
- the processes of political socialization in Canada;
- the various interest groups that generate public opinion and the activities of these groups that make demands on the Canadian political system;
- the structure and functions of the Canadian political system, including its political parties, its multi-tiered constitutional framework, its ability to handle the demands made on it, and the problems within the system resulting in any structural or functional defects;
- the ways in which the results of government decisions are received by and affect Canadians and their willingness to give continuing support to the political community, its institutions, and authorities;
- the essential elements of the Canadian economic system and the multitude of interests and diversities within the system that are the prime causes of conflict and tension in Canada;
- the efforts by Canadians to define common goals and the methods by which these goals may be achieved; and
- the willingness of Canadians to abide by the rules as well as the frustrations and ambitions that lead to the abuse of democratic understandings.

From this point on, the term "the Canadian environment" will be used in this book to describe the totality of the basic features of Canada, the interactions between them and their far-ranging effects. This is, of course, a much broader interpretation of the word environment than that used in biology or ecology. This broad interpretation is useful in civic education because it permits a differentiation between two major components of the Canadian political community: its environment, and the structure and functioning of its political system. Thus it is possible to develop separate, preliminary studies of the Canadian environment and the Canadian political system, although ultimately the interlocking relationships between the two are essential to an understanding of Canada.

CANADA STUDIES: THE FOUR COMPONENTS

From the preceding description of civic education and the Canadian political community it is apparent that Canada Studies includes four separate but interrelated components.

1. The Canadian environment. The emphasis here is on the five basic features of Canada, their origins, a descriptive analysis of them, the interactions between them and, in general terms, their impact on the Canadian political community. Students should understand that the basic features are the major sources of diversity in Canada; that they are strong factors in the formation of public opinion and the differences in viewpoint on public issues in various parts of the country; that they generate most of the problems of continuing concern to Canadians and cause social tension; and that they substantially influence the structure and functioning of Canada's political and economic systems. All other Canada Studies should be approached with the background knowledge provided by a careful analysis of the basic features of this country.

2. **The structure and functioning of government.** This aspect of civic education includes a study of the origins and the present structure of the Canadian federal system of government; the ways in which it responds to public opinions; its power to take initiatives in policy formation and implementation without prodding from the public; federal-provincial relations as a reflection of both confrontation and cooperation; the roles of political parties as a major form of political activity; the strengths and weaknesses of the system and its ability to handle conflict and tension. Less emphasis is placed on a factual description of the structure of government and much more on functions, issues, interest groups, public opinions, aggregation of public needs and demands by political parties, and inputs to the political system and feedbacks from the system to society.

Students should understand that the Canadian federal system of government is based on a delicate balance between divergencies of language, ethnic origin, culture, economics, and geography. Thus, the challenge for federalism is to adjust to change so that cultural, economic, linguistic, regional, and other interests are nourished within a shared political community. This raises questions concerning the finding of common social goals and reaching a consensus on the means for achieving them in a society characterized by diversity, huge distances, and vastly differing viewpoints. Also included are the fundamental principles and understandings of democratic societies, the rights and obligations of individuals, and the willingness to accept or reject them.

3. **The essential characteristics and functioning of the Canadian economic system.** The emphasis in this aspect of civic education is primarily on the complex economic effects of the basic features of Canada. This approach is designed to give students a reasonably detailed overview of the major components of Canada's economy and the interrelationships between them, with as little economic theory as is necessary. Some of the most important fundamental questions facing Canadians are economic ones arising from inequalities of income, possessions, status, and power between individuals, groups, and regions. Such issues range from debates about the role of governments in economic life, to concern for resource use and conservation, to striving for an appropriate balance between the main sectors of the economy, to anxieties about employment, inflation, and stability in economic life. The purpose here is to give students sufficient information about the structure and functioning of the Canadian economy so they may understand economic questions of this kind.

4. **Public issues in Canada.** Public issues are questions or problems of sufficient magnitude to arouse the interest and concern of Canadians. These questions

have become a part of the political community; they form elements in public opinion; they are visible through the media, public debate, committees of investigation, the platforms of political parties, opinion surveys, and legislative debates.

Agreement on public issues in a democratic society is exceedingly difficult to attain and frequently public issues provoke controversy and tension requiring political activity for their attempted resolution. It is important to emphasize that the word "problem" does not have only negative meanings. Problems are simply the challenges faced by a society; their effects can be either positive or negative depending on the wisdom and understanding used by the members of a political community in attempting to resolve them.

The words "public issues", "problems", "challenges" may be correctly interpreted to mean either a single major question or a general area of concern in which a number of related questions or problems arise. The objective here is to provide a broad overview of the challenges facing Canadians and to emphasize general areas of concern rather than detailed studies of particular problems. Furthermore, the emphasis is on issues that are national or international in scope. The point has already been made and merits repetition that many questions of great importance to Canadians are regional or national symptoms of world-wide problems whose magnitude transcends domestic issues.

Since problems are generated by the interactions of the basic features of Canada, since many of the most critical ones are economic in nature, and since all of them require the use of political processes for their solution, it is clear that the study of public issues should be regarded as the climactic part of civic education. The students' previously acquired knowledge and understandings of the Canadian environment and of the political and economic systems should be broadened and synthesized by studying examples of conflict, and conflict resolution within the Canadian political community.

SCOPE AND SEQUENCE FOR CANADA STUDIES

Improvement in the quality of studies of Canada requires that students have the opportunity to study all four components of Canada Studies during their secondary school years, preceded by an elementary school social studies program which is designed specifically for Canadian children. Subsequent chapters present the emphasis that should be given to each of these elements of a comprehensive Canada Studies program, and indicate how each component is intimately related to all others.

This is not to claim, however, that there is only one possible sequence curriculum organization for Canada Studies. Particularly because of the existence of provincial jurisdictions in Canadian education, there must be different methods of organizing studies of Canada to meet the distinctive curriculum needs of the various provinces. It is possible, for example, to envision the concurrent study of the Canadian environment, the political and economic systems, and public issues with the development of simpler understandings of all components in the earlier years, followed by the more complex understandings in the later years.

15

Canadian curriculum specialists, using the general approach described in this book, are quite capable of devising courses in Canada Studies for several grade levels, with scope and sequences appropriate to the varieties of Canadian educational systems.

Nevertheless, there is one curriculum structure for Canada Studies that seems particularly desirable and applicable to all school systems in Canada. This approach would call for a new orientation to elementary school social studies which places particular emphasis on basic citizenship education and the study of Canadian communities. This study would be followed at the beginning of secondary school by a study of the total environment of Canada under the title, the Canadian Environment. In the middle years of secondary school, students would examine both the Canadian Political System and the Canadian Economic System. With this background of understandings, students in the last years of secondary school would then examine Canadian Public Issues. This approach would allow students throughout Canada to develop a comprehensive understanding of their own society in a coherent and orderly fashion.

This approach to studies of Canada may appear to some educators to be too difficult for many students or too time-consuming in an already crowded school day. It need not be so, and should not be if it is not unduly detailed. As already indicated, its purpose is to provide all students by the time they graduate from secondary school with a broad understanding of the nature, institutional structure, and functioning of Canadian society and with a sound method of examining public issues. Such an understanding is adaptable to different intellectual capacities of students. The specific understandings that are explained in detail in subsequent chapters should be seen as optimums – what the best students should know and understand about Canada by the time they complete secondary school. There is ample scope for teachers to make selections and adjustments in degrees of difficulty to meet the different capacities of students and to acknowledge the practical reality that other studies must have their share of the school day. At the same time, this approach should ensure that even the least able ones achieve minimum levels of understanding of Canada. Indeed, to overlook the value and importance of Canada Studies for all Canadian students or to claim that our young people are incapable of acquiring the kind of education required for responsible citizenship is to deny a fundamental assumption of democracy.

It might also be claimed that this approach places an almost exclusive emphasis on the study of Canada in political terms and ignores the important perceptions of the Canadian experience made by our writers and artists. This claim is a misinterpretation of the intent of the approach proposed in this book; the creative insights to be found in the works of Canada's writers and artists can contribute through this approach to a more complete understanding of Canadian society. But it is important to recognize that a study of Canada which does not give prominence to Canada as a political community will not encourage participative citizenship – the long-term objective of Canada Studies.

Finally, there is the long-standing fear in Canadian education of being too parochial and ignoring the fact that students must also be educated as world citizens. The Canada Studies program proposed here consistently makes the point that Canada must always be viewed in the world context; many of the

16

Canadian Public Issues, for example, are world problems as well as Canadian ones. Also, Canadian schools at present are so far away from being too Canadian that the problem is not a real one. Canadian schools are not yet sufficiently Canadian.

CHAPTER III

Studying Canada in the Elementary Years

Education for citizenship – for an active role in the life of society – begins before the child enters elementary school. In their neighborhood games and in play at home, children learn quickly about disagreement and conflict and they develop their first techniques for settling differences. At home they are exposed to rules and authority, and they learn how decisions are made. In casual but important ways, civic education in at least a limited way has started. On school entry, this education, primarily through social studies, should become less casual but no less important. Indeed it is the foundation for all subsequent years of study.

Social studies during the elementary school years have traditionally had several important objectives. One has been the development of social awareness; in other words, the fostering of a system of values with respect to one's fellow man, the growth of understanding of social relationships, and respect for one's physical and cultural heritage. A second objective has been an education in the rights and duties of citizenship. Thirdly, there has been an introductory study of societies, cultures, and ways of living of a variety of peoples past and present. All of these objectives are valid in their own right; yet none of them requires elementary school children even to identify Canada as the political community in which they must later become participating citizens. It is legitimate to ask, however, whether Canadian elementary school social studies, while pursuing objectives common to social studies elsewhere, should begin the preparation of Canadian children for active involvement in Canadian public life.

The answer to this question must be an affirmative one. This is not to suggest that Canadian children need more social studies than children elsewhere; it is not the quantity of social studies that is critical, but the orientation that such studies should take.

This need for Canadian citizenship education is strongly supported in studies by Canadian social scientists and educators, who have recently developed a particular interest in attempting to determine what and how young people learn about life in society. Few of them have had the temerity as yet to draw any firm generalizations about the manner in which elementary school children acquire their knowledge, attitudes, beliefs, and values about people in society. There are, however, a number of tentative findings about the processes of political socialization that argue in favor of an early start to positive civic education.*

Periodic surveys of the political knowledge of Canadian children (or at least of their ability to memorize "political" information) have produced discouraging results. Children at the end of the elementary school, like many Canadian adults, do badly at identifying names in the news, confuse people and positions and societies, and seem woefully ignorant of important details of the major public issues of the day. To rub salt into the wound, researchers are dismayed that many Canadian children know more of the folklore of the United States than of Canada and are better versed in American political life than in Canadian. If it is of any consolation, Canadian educators are not alone in facing problems such as these. Indeed, the indications are that this kind of political misinformation is universal, differing only in degree from one society to another. Perhaps elementary school children anywhere should not be expected to acquire a fingertip knowledge of the personalities, events, and issues of a world or society which they are only gradually entering.

However, the result of surveys cannot be interpreted to mean that young children are incapable of becoming politically or socially sensitive or of mastering some basic understandings of how societies function. Rather, they should be interpreted to mean that children, like most adults, do not readily retain isolated, incoherent, and meaningless data. Several studies have revealed that even very young children are indeed able to respond intelligently and consistently to questions about persons, objects, symbols, and institutions that are political in character, and that they can and do make perceptive judgments on social questions and political issues – if their education is so oriented.

Virtually all research tends to support the view that children begin school with very positive attitudes toward and perceptions of their country. Examination of young children's writings and drawings reinforce the view that young children have a positive and joyful curiosity about their world. The same studies also tend to indicate that, by adolescence, children's perceptions of Canada remain neither so common nor so positive; of particular significance is the finding that cleavages between the views of francophone and anglophone youngsters regarding Canada have become evident by adolescence. Other studies carried out from Alberta to Nova Scotia seem to indicate that students gradually become more aware of their provincial or regional identities and, in some cases, less positive toward Canada as a whole as they proceed through the school years.

Several interpretations can be given to these findings. One is that, as they

---

* Reports or reviews of recent research on the political socialization of Canadian children will be found in: E. Zureik and R. M. Pike, eds., *Socialization and Values in Canadian Society, Volume I: Political Socialization* (Toronto: McClelland & Stewart, 1975); J. H. Pammett and M. S. Whittington, eds., *Foundations of Political Culture; Political Socialization in Canada* (Toronto: Macmillan of Canada, 1976); G. S. Tomkins, "Political Socialization Research and Canadian Studies," *The Canadian Journal of Education*, vol. 2, no. 1 (1977): 83–91.

grow up, young Canadians gradually take on the perspectives of their elders, most of whom have long been socialized to a provincial or regional culture more than to a nation-wide one. Another is that the schools of Canada have simply ignored the Canadian reality, reinforced regional and local perspectives, and allowed the youth of Canada to grow up indifferent to public affairs in their own larger society. Whatever the interpretation, it is clear that the future of Canadian society as a diverse country with enormous challenges to its well-being, if not survival, is dim indeed unless the schools of Canada assume a much greater responsibility for positive citizenship education as Canadians.

Nonetheless, what the schools should do and when they should do it are not identified with any clarity. How the social perceptions of young Canadians are developed, and the relative significance of the family, peer group, school, church, and media as instruments of political socialization are not clearly defined.

What is evident is that all these agencies influence the political sensitivity of children to some extent, and that the school's influence is probably potent. Several observers have noted that the influence of the school can be particularly powerful as much for the way in which it operates as for the specific subject matter that it teaches. Some point to the fact that the very formality of the school as a place whose specific role is learning enhances the legitimacy of what is taught. Most Canadians of an older generation, for example, can remember being in awe of teachers and clinging to their words, simply because they were teachers. And many teachers know that they have used rightly and consciously their positions to persuade or require their students to study what children would otherwise have viewed as inconsequential.

Some social scientists have placed particular emphasis on the fact that the school is commonly the first formal setting in which a child meets large numbers of other children on a basis of equality. They note that the manner in which children are treated by their peers and by persons in authority, and the manner in which disagreements and social relationships are managed, may serve as powerful and lasting models for behavior in all large social settings. Whether children are streamed by ability or grouped by age, how children's desks or work spaces are arranged in classrooms, and how student performance is graded or evaluated have been cited as subtle yet likely powerful influences on the child's perceptions of role, hierarchy, status, and decision-making processes in the larger society.

Quite apart from these less tangible potential influences of the school, there are two quite definite and related sources of impact on the social perceptions of Canadian children: one is the curriculum or course of studies, and the other is the textbook or the learning materials.

It is hardly likely that children in Canada will develop positive attitudes toward Canada, or wish to participate actively in Canadian public life, or acquire at least a basic understanding of the nature of Canadian society, if these subjects do not constitute a significant part of the school curriculum. For example, if Canada as a whole is not a subject of study in some fashion at any time in the elementary years (and in many parts of Canada this is currently so) how can we expect that children's positive perceptions of Canada will be fostered and developed in these critical years? Similarly, if little attention is paid in the formal elementary school curriculum to education for citizenship, there is little likelihood that children, at a time when values and attitudes are being formed, will acquire patterns of behavior conducive to participative citizenship. Surely, if understanding Canada and preparing for active participation in Canadian public life are reasonable objectives of the school, they will not be realized unless knowledge of Canada as a whole and training for citizenship are given some prominence in these crucial early school years.

While only supportive to the curriculum and to teaching, textbooks and learning materials have a measurable impact on what students learn. There are numerous reports revealing that textbooks in Canadian schools fall short on several counts: textbook authorities insist that school materials shy away from controversy, and in an effort not to offend anyone, they become simply bland; in an effort to reach the widest possible student audience, they dare not overestimate the reading ability of children or deal with issues or ideas of any complexity; they are commonly biased toward middle-class and single-culture values, with only token recognition of the rich diversity of the Canadian experience and the widely differing views that Canadians hold on so many public issues. It is bad enough that children in Atlantic Canadian schools must make substantial use of materials developed by Ontario authors with little sensitivity to the Atlantic experience and little regard for Western Canadian development (or spin-off American books in "Canadianized" editions); but it is little short of tragic when children throughout Canada are presented with a homogenized, inoffensive, standardized view of a country that is much more characterized by diversity than by uniformity. In short, both official courses of studies and most textbooks have tended to fail by default.

If the school can have such a negative influence, as some have claimed, logically it can also have a positive one. So much depends upon what is done in the elementary school, and how it is done. It is futile, however, to consider what should be done, when it should be done, and how it should be done, until there is the conviction that something must be done – and seriously. The truth of the matter is that Canadian schools in the seventies have swung back to a preoccupation with the "basics" of education. Despite public insistence that schools do a better job of preparing students for adult citizenship, Canadian educators have not yet seen fit to identify citizenship education for Canadian society as one of the basic elements of the elementary school curriculum. Lip service and curriculum guidelines aside, elementary school educators are still relegating social studies to a second level of importance.

In fact, part of the contemporary elementary school reality in Canada is that any form of citizenship education is greeted with either indifference or scepticism by many elementary educators as some repugnant form of jingoism. To others, it may not be so viewed but the possibility of achieving something significant at the elementary level is doubted. Until attitudes such as these are confronted squarely, new approaches to elementary curriculum development hold little promise. The needs of Canadian society indicate that learning about societies and how they function ought to be basic to all elementary education in Canada and that learning about Canadian social realities ought to constitute the predominant part of these studies.

22

This is not a criticism of elementary school teachers as much as an indictment of the understanding and support they have received. Most teachers receive only the most generalized and platitudinous guidelines for the construction of their own programs. Schoolbook publishers try in vain to find common threads to programs in the same school district, let alone throughout a province, and then throw up their hands in dismay at their inability to supply a market that they know should be there. Teachers responsible for preparing work in several subjects day after day understandably let social studies slide or spend a disproportionate time on their own favorite topics because neither they nor their students have the materials with which they might do otherwise. And most teachers have not had the opportunity to study much about Canada beyond their last survey course in the History of Canada back in their university years. They have been exposed in their teacher education to methods and theories of instruction, but many have had little recent academic substance to which this pedagogical preparation can be applied.

CANADA IN THE PRIMARY YEARS

A realistic plan for the initial formal preparation of young Canadians for participation in the public affairs of Canada calls for a start at the beginning of elementary school and a continuation through the elementary years. A fresh and pertinent orientation to elementary school social studies, in particular, can be developed if there is a special focus on those aspects of Canada Studies, as sketched in Chapter 2, which are appropriate to the elementary school years, regardless of the specific content of the social studies program at each grade level.

The categorization of types of learnings as knowledge, skills, and attitudes is a common practice of teachers; it is also almost as common for them in their teaching to give emphasis to knowledge first, skills second, and the development of attitudes and values last. For this reason, it is important to stress that learnings about Canada in the primary grades should be more concerned with the development of attitudes than with the accumulation of information; positive attitudes toward participative citizenship and toward Canadians from coast to coast should be a far more predominant preoccupation of teachers than the mastery of Canadian facts or the development of understandings in any profound or sophisticated sense.

In the primary grades, learnings are particularly desirable in the following areas:

– community participation;
– public affairs versus private, family, or special group affairs; and
– public controversy as a normal and constructive social reality.

Dimensions of these learnings appropriate to the primary grades are sketched below.

LEARNING ABOUT COMMUNITY PARTICIPATION

In every province of Canada, the social studies program in the earliest years of school is devoted to a study of the immediate social environment of the child;

the family, the neighborhood, the community. Usually this study takes the form of an examination of the roles of persons and institutions with which the child will come in contact: the fireman, the policeman, the storekeeper, the mayor, a church, and a local industry, to name a few. Depending upon how this examination is conducted, it can be particularly good as preparation for Canada Studies; the critical element in it should be the emphasis on the community or neighborhood as a dynamic, functional social unit rather than as a static collection of interesting people and things.

Children in the first years of school should not only view the persons and positions and institutions of their community but should also begin to examine how they relate to one another – a key aspect of Canada Studies. At a very young age, children should begin to learn why people come to live together in "communities": not only for companionship but also to have services which they could not otherwise have. Children should examine their communities with a view to understanding what roles different people play in their community and how these roles produce a social unit which functions in such a way as to provide all members of the community with benefits they would not otherwise have.

LEARNING ABOUT PUBLIC AFFAIRS

In these first years, children should also be exposed, through the study of their own community, to some of the basic responsibilities of being a member of a community. A fundamental responsibility to be introduced is that of participation in the affairs of the community; children should learn at an early age that the right to express one's views – or to vote – is part and parcel of being an adult member of their community. It is part of growing up; it is a responsibility not to be ignored. In every community there are issues which come to public attention that can serve to introduce to young children, and then to reinforce for them, one of the essential characteristics of public life in Canada.

The distinction between the public affairs of a community and those matters that are specific to a person or to a family or to only a special group is not beyond the comprehension of the child in the first years of school and it is important that this distinction be made as early as possible. A community plan to build a playground to serve a neighborhood rather than a single family, or a decision on where to construct a hockey rink, or even to put in sidewalks, are examples of opportunities for teachers to help students to understand what public affairs are and how they affect the citizens of their community.

LEARNING ABOUT CONTROVERSY

It is also not unrealistic to propose that children in the first years of school be introduced to the idea of public controversy; in fact, it is desirable to do so at a time when children have such positive perceptions of their social world. To most adults, controversy, issues, and problems have negative connotations. The example above of a decision to build a playground provides opportunities for children to see that people do not always agree on what is best, to see that a community decision is made frequently by adults by means of voting, and to see that people in their community abide by the rules even when they may not personally agree with a decision of the majority of the community. The study of the playground example need not take on disagreeable overtones; it can just as well be used to demonstrate that public controversy is a normal and frequently positive fact of community life that can allow a community to reach new levels of achievement. It is the idea of public controversy as a potentially constructive community force, if it is dealt with as a challenge rather than something destructive, that can help to build for young children social attitudes fundamental for effective civic education.

In the primary grades, then, foundations for Canada Studies can be built in several ways: by giving attention to the study of the local community as a dynamic social reality; by providing an introduction to the responsibilities of citizenship on a scale that is comprehensible to the young child; by an initial development of the meaning of public affairs and their importance to communities; and by a perception of public controversy as a normal and constructive community activity. All of this can be done without major changes in the current content of most primary grade social studies; a change of emphasis rather than content is all that is required.

CANADA IN THE MIDDLE AND UPPER YEARS

From the middle to later years of elementary school, there is no pattern of social studies consistent throughout the provinces of Canada. In some provinces, curriculum guidelines place emphasis on local, regional, or "other community" studies with an accent on historical, geographical, and sociological components; in others, emphasis is placed on the study of "themes" such as interdependence, cooperation, and change; some later elementary social studies remain entirely locally based, while in other cases children study people in communities throughout the world; in some instances, all social studies are strictly contemporary, but in others a significant historical element is included. In all cases, however, curriculum guidelines are quite limited (frequently to statements of broad objectives rather than specific content) and teachers are given full responsibility (frequently expressed as the professional freedom) to design and implement their own social studies courses. This decentralization of curriculum design and development to the level of the individual classroom teacher, accompanied by the elimination of the provincially prescribed textbook or learning materials, has meant that although teachers have largely been given the opportunity to do whatever they want in social studies, most have been given neither a framework nor the learning materials to do very much effectively.

To illustrate, a detailed survey of social studies in elementary schools throughout Canada would probably reveal that Canadian Indians are by far the most popular topic in the middle and later years of elementary school; Indian crafts may be a theme for a child in Grade 4; that same child may well learn about canoe construction in a Grade 5 project; again in Grade 6 aspects of Indian life might be encountered in the study of the world's nomadic peoples. Almost as popular have been the explorers. Children travel for a week with Champlain, suffer for a period of time with Radisson or Samuel Hearne, and share Henry Hudson's horrors.

These illustrations are obvious caricatures, and in some cases quite unfair.

25

Nevertheless, they are not far off the mark for many children in Canada and they suggest reasons for the level of insensitivity and ignorance among young Canadians to their own society, its past and, more important, the present.

Quite literally, thousands of children in Canada have progressed through elementary school with only disconnected snippets about their world and their own society beyond the local community. Many children complete elementary school with little knowledge about the most basic aspects of living in a larger society, with little sense of oneness with others beyond their own environment, and with little inkling that such knowledge and such sensitivity are worthwhile. Furthermore, what is studied in the last year of elementary school may only accidentally relate either to studies in earlier years or to what will follow in secondary school. It is quite common for students entering high school not to have been exposed to any coherence or progression in studies of their own society and their world. A great deal of interesting information about a broad range of topics may well have been the legacy of the elementary school, but it has rarely been organized to result in the development of any significant understandings or attitudes or values that can carry over to studies in later grades.

From the middle to last years of elementary school, foundations for Canada Studies additional to those indicated in the primary years and consistent with the learning abilities of older children can be built; they can serve not only as a preparation for later, more systematic studies of Canada as a political community, but also as a means of bringing coherence and progression to later elementary social studies.

In the middle and upper years of elementary school, learnings are particularly desirable in the following areas:

– community life throughout Canada and the world;
– Canada as a political community;
– Canada in the world community;
– participative citizenship;
– compromise and consensus; and
– representative government.

Dimensions of these learnings appropriate to these grade levels are sketched below.

COMMUNITY LIFE THROUGHOUT CANADA AND THE WORLD

Having already studied their own community and how it operates, in the middle elementary grades children should begin to study life in other communities. A common question faced by curriculum specialists in this regard has been: What other communities? To some, the answer has been that it doesn't really matter as long as children have the opportunity to examine life-styles and cultures different from their own. Others have argued that children should be exposed to a systematic study of peoples in quite contrasting physical and cultural settings throughout the world so that they will recognize themselves as a part of a world community of peoples of great diversity. This answer has resulted in children studying life in Norway, Egypt, Greece, and Iceland – but not in parts of Canada.

Children in Canadian elementary schools, from the middle to the later years, should have continuing opportunity to study peoples in various communities and physical settings, and most particularly communities in Canada. Such an approach can provide for children the same range of life-styles and physical and cultural settings as would a more global approach, but has the additional advantages of reinforcing the child's own identity as a Canadian and displaying for the first time the diversity of Canadian society, a fundamental concept of Canada Studies. Children who live in or near any of the cosmopolitan urban centres of Canada have ideal opportunities close at hand to examine several aspects of Canadian diversity.

The importance of children's growth in awareness of themselves as Canadians – of sharing a land, traditions, and a culture with other Canadians – cannot be overestimated. The specific dimensions of this awareness will develop with teaching and over time; what is desirable at this formative stage is the attitudinal development which says to young Canadians wherever they may live that they have much in common with others in this vast and varied country. Rural Canadian children should come to identify with their urban counterparts, West with East, French-speaking with English-speaking and those who speak neither, advantaged with disadvantaged, newcomers with those whose family roots are well established in Canada. Children anywhere in Canada should come to know, at least in a preliminary way, children elsewhere in Canada, so that they can come to a first appreciation that all of Canada is theirs – an important part of them, their share of the world community of peoples, their legacy from earlier Canadians. Building a sense of "I am Canadian and these people in other parts of Canada are part of me" is a legitimate role of the elementary school.

In the study of Canadian communities in the middle and upper elementary grades it is particularly important to expose children to life-styles in parts of Canada remote from where they live. Students should not limit their studies to other adjacent and similar communities, or proceed simply from the study of their own community, to other adjacent communities, to their own provincial studies, and then to studies of their own region. Indeed, the significance of concepts such as provinces and regions is far more suitable for later study in a different context. This "expanding horizons" approach, while both logical and pedagogically defensible, is far more likely to establish and reinforce the very attitudes and values that Canada Studies will later attempt to modify and balance. Students in Central Canada must learn about Canadians in coastal settings, children in southern Ontario must learn about Canadians in the Far North, and young Canadians raised in anglophone milieux must learn about their counterparts in cosmopolitan communities and in French-language settings.

The approach to community studies proposed here might be viewed as unduly ambitious. Whether it is depends upon the emphases given to these studies. For them to be supportive to the development of pan-Canadian understanding, only three elements need attention in the study of each community: *how* people live in that community; *why* they live as they do; and *why* they are dependent upon people in other communities.

Children of elementary school age, with or without teaching, come to recognize differences among all kinds of people. They see differences of wealth, of customs, of color, of interests, to mention only a few. What they also need to see and come to appreciate is that all people, regardless of differences, have had, now have, and will continue to have a broad range of common needs, hopes, and interests – for food, clothing, shelter, recreation, opportunities for self-expression. Over the later elementary years and in a variety of settings, students should come to recognize that they have much in common with other people wherever and however they may live; this sense of similarity to, and community with, all peoples should receive continuing emphasis on these years.

They should equally begin to understand why people whom they learn about have evident differences. They should learn that, apart from similarities, people in different places and times quite normally and naturally express and meet their needs and wants in various ways – that people live and have lived differently because they have different resources available to them, different traditions, different environments, and different forms of expression. This study of other peoples, although interesting and valuable as a purely descriptive exercise, should be directed primarily to helping children appreciate *why* similarities and differences exist. The study of peoples in elementary grades should deter children from presuming that people who are different from themselves are odd or strange or that one way of living is inherently better than any other; rather, a respect for diversity of expression with a fundamental similarity of need should be a dominant objective of elementary social studies – an objective most compatible with the purpose of Canada Studies.

CANADA AS A POLITICAL COMMUNITY

It is not important at this stage for children to be able to use the term "political community" as defined in Chapter 2. But the basic appreciation that Canada as a totality is the political community of Canadian children should be initiated in these years. Beginning with the primary grade notion of their own local community as the immediate larger social reality of the child, and building from there to the examination of other larger and different social settings throughout the country, children can and should begin to recognize "Canada" as the composite of several smaller "communities" or interest groups based on neighborhood, region, ethnic origin, religion, language, occupation, economic status, or other characteristics. They should equally come to a first recognition that all these other communities exist within recognized, clearly defined geographic boundaries, have a number of shared institutions, and work out their common goals and differences according to an established set of rules for social behavior. Thus, in effect if not in words, they constitute a political community.

CANADA IN THE WORLD COMMUNITY

It is legitimate to contend that an exclusive preoccupation with Canada and things Canadian throughout the elementary years is too narrow and chauvinistic. Indeed, one of the major emphases of Canada Studies in later years should be that Canadians have been too inward-looking, so preoccupied with internal questions that they have not put larger world questions such as famine, human rights, and energy shortages into proper perspective. Canadian children in elementary school should certainly learn about people in lands far away in time

28

and space, but this should not be at the expense of learning about Canada and other Canadians. Ideally, after the primary grades, children should be helped to identify themselves as Canadians – to know that Canada is their political community – and to begin to appreciate that it is through their political community that they can make their contributions and fulfill their obligations to world society. Balanced by studies in other subject areas and at other grade levels as well as by out-of-school influences, a predominance to Canada in the elementary school is not likely to present much risk of obstructing a balanced preparation of the child for world citizenship. Indeed, an elementary education which does not place sufficient emphasis on understanding Canada is an imbalanced education for Canadian children.

PARTICIPATIVE CITIZENSHIP

Another emphasis in social studies in the middle and later elementary years should be an extension of the initiation into participative citizenship begun in the primary grades. At the higher grade levels, children's earlier introduction to their own community as a dynamic social reality can be strengthened by examining in operation the other communities that they should encounter in these years; the distinction between public affairs and private or small-group affairs can be further developed; the idea of public controversy as a potentially constructive community force can be further illustrated; the importance of the right to vote can be reinforced. These years also lend themselves to the development of new citizenship understandings closely related to the objectives of Canada Studies.

Students should now be helped to understand that members of communities, however large or small, develop rules that indicate how the members of these communities are expected to conduct their public affairs – in fact, how these communities shall be governed. They should learn that not all communities within Canada and within world society are governed in the same ways (and they may even compare and contrast forms of government). They should learn that, in Canada, the members of a local community establish some of their own rules (or laws) but that other laws are established by and with people from other communities and are then binding on all these communities. They might learn that, in some places of the world today, and virtually everywhere at some time, laws have been established without the participation of the people who will be bound by them. In effect, rudimentary notions of the rule of law as distinct from the rule of person, so fundamental to an understanding of the Canadian political system, can be developed at the elementary grade level.

COMPROMISE AND CONSENSUS

Children in the middle and upper elementary grades should also be introduced to the ideas of compromise and consensus, as normal and positive methods of dealing with matters where there are differences of opinion among peoples and where decisions affecting all must be made. Too often the word compromise is presented as a weak-kneed response to difference of views, while the word consensus, if encountered at all, conveys a negative sense. In these formative years, children can learn that compromise is an essential ingredient of reasonable social existence and commonly a most satisfactory and reputable solution where there are strong differences of opinion. It is not beyond the capability of children of these ages to consider the alternatives to compromise, to recognize its merits, and to see a relationship between rule of law and compromise.

Similarly, for children to begin to appreciate the concepts of equality and sharing in a social setting, they should have opportunities to examine the meaning and importance of consensus. Having examined several Canadian communities with very different life-styles and settings, children can begin to understand that the search for what will be acceptable to most if not all of them is a desirable way of respecting the rights and interests of a great diversity of peoples and communities, even though the most acceptable course of action may not be entirely satisfactory to any single community in Canada.

REPRESENTATIVE GOVERNMENT

It is at this stage as well that children should go beyond an introduction to the idea of voting to two further ideas so fundamental to effective citizenship education: the idea of office-holding or leadership, and the idea of informed public opinion. Children of these ages can well appreciate that citizens vote not only on specific issues or affairs but that they also vote for persons who can act on their behalf on a whole range of public matters. Government by elected representatives, though not necessarily in those words, can be understood in a preliminary way by quite young children. Indeed, they can practise representative government in their own classrooms, and assess at least some of its advantages and limitations. Because the principle of representation is so crucial to the character of Canadian political life, an initial study in several settings is well worthwhile at this school level.

More difficult, but attainable and desirable, is the development of a first understanding of the impact of public opinion. Children should learn that a citizen's right to vote in public affairs requires that the citizen be informed about the question or the person at issue. An extension of this understanding to include some appreciation of the need for all citizens to be continually active as well as knowledgeable in matters of public interest is a legitimate objective in elementary school.

A CASE FOR CANADIAN HISTORY AND GEOGRAPHY

A more formal yet introductory study of the history and geography of Canada as a whole in the last years of elementary school is another means of initiating students into Canada Studies, despite the recent unpopularity of this approach among curriculum experts. Two arguments have been made in recent years to question the validity of this approach. One has been that Canada is really just an abstraction – a symbol – for young people who have not experienced Canada, and therefore the term cannot have any real meaning for them. The second is that children's sense of time and place is very unrefined – that things beyond yesterday are history and anything beyond tomorrow is "the future" – and thus the past and the distant are really quite meaningless.

To the first argument – that Canada is but an incomprehensible abstraction – one can counter that, to the elementary student the same might be said about the terms Ontario or Montreal or Egypt. In fact, because of the impact of television, Canada is likely to be less incomprehensible and more familiar than many other terms and place names. In any event, any abstraction will only become meaningful and personalized over time and with deliberate teaching with this end in mind. The study of Canada should, of course, be preceded by a study of local settings which have personal meaning to a child; but it could continue, at the end of elementary school, with the structure and sequence that can be provided by the history and geography of Canada.

The argument that the child's sense of time and space are quite unrefined, although correct, misses the point when it is extended to say that history and geography go beyond the capacity of elementary school children. Elementary school history can capitalize on a child's sense of continuity – which is quite refined – and which serves as one of the real attractions of good children's literature. Analogously, the study of geography provides its own structure, and helps children to develop spatial relationships. Of course, the very first studies of people in society should be contemporary ones; senses of sequence, continuity, space, and extended time periods will develop with maturation and teaching. It is a challenge, but not an insurmountable one, for elementary teachers to bring children to this point.

There are good geography textbooks written for Canadian school children. They are good to the extent that they are designed to develop understandings of the reciprocal relationships between the land and the peoples of Canada. They are good to the extent that they give focus to Canada as a whole rather than merely to its parts. They are good to the extent that they reinforce the geographic relationships of Canada to the rest of the world.

It is more difficult to identify elementary level history books which do justice to the development of Canada. This difficulty arises in part because different parts of Canada have quite different histories. Atlantic Canada, central Canada, Western Canada, and northern Canada had quite different starting points and evolutions and, while it is possible to tie together the strands of all, it is usual for a story of Canada to place disproportionate emphasis on only one part of the full story.

The difficulty is magnified by the fact that Canadian histories for children have tended to follow the lead of Canadian historians by giving particular attention to Canada's political and constitutional development. Constitutional history is devoid of the humanity and flair and excitement that should characterize upper elementary studies. Without discounting its importance, political and constitutional history is simply not the stuff of elementary school.

However, a social history of Canada which tells the story of how Canadian ways of living have developed – a story which features individuals and groups in Canada and their changing life-styles – is indeed appropriate to the upper years of elementary school. Such a history can be full of the drama that is important in these years; it can also establish the settings within which political and constitutional developments can be examined and understood in later years.

The definitive history of Canada has not been written nor will it be written; equally, a child's history of Canada that finds general acceptance throughout Canada will not be written. Nevertheless, a story of Canada which acknowledges the different paths by which Canadians have come to the present is a means of developing both a sense of continuity and a sense of the wholeness of Canada.

With these reservations in mind, it nevertheless seems valuable to begin a study of Canadian history and geography in the later elementary years. Such a study, which places particular emphasis on the social and physical dimensions of these disciplines rather than on the constitutional and scientific dimensions, can do much to prepare students for the study of the first component of Canada Studies, The Canadian Environment.

EDUCATION FOR CITIZENSHIP VERSUS CIVICS

To develop the citizenship understandings indicated above does not require the formal study of civics; indeed, examination of structures and formal processes of government is an undesirable approach at these levels of schooling.

There are other approaches more appropriate to the elementary school. One is to capitalize on the exposure to public affairs that virtually all children receive through television, if not radio and newspapers as well; children can benefit from discussions, debates, and analyses of public issues in the news. Another approach is the study of public affairs in their own communities. Local issues both large and small provide realistic opportunities for young children to analyse political attitudes and behavior in settings with which they are familiar. Yet a third approach to the acquisition of initial familiarity with and competency in tasks of citizenship is to capitalize on the everyday situations encountered by the children themselves which involve their own group decisions and choices. At home they encounter rules about their own conduct and at least sometimes share in the decisions made; at school and in the neighborhood they encounter other rules determined in different ways and they are involved in choices about who will play on what teams and how the teams will be selected. The informal analysis of such political situations are child-related opportunities to develop understandings and senses of group responsibility and social obligation, of far more benefit than memorization of legalistic descriptions of government practices or abstract political concepts or the superficial perusal of customs of peoples of far-away times and place. By a combination of such approaches, elementary school children can come to appreciate that participative citizenship is not associated exclusively with remote governments and large, impersonal institutions but also with their own everyday lives – another fundamental concept of Canada Studies.

PREPARATION FOR CANADA STUDIES

The purpose of social studies in Canadian elementary schools is not to prepare children for later and more complex studies; elementary school social studies have their own legitimate rationale consistent with the learning abilities of younger children and compatible with objectives of other subject areas at this level of schooling. However, by selecting the content for elementary social studies in full recognition of the fact that the children are members of a distinctively Canadian society and will be expected by that society to participate actively in its public affairs as adults, curriculum designers and teachers can concurrently achieve the general objectives of elementary social studies and begin the preparation for active citizenship in their own society.

By the end of elementary school, children in Canada should have developed a real sense of personal identification with Canada as a whole, with Canadians throughout the country, and with Canada's physical and cultural heritage – as a legitimate balance to, but not a substitute for, the tendencies in Canada to view public issues in local, provincial, or regional perspectives. Children throughout Canada, primarily through the study of community life in all parts of Canada, should have begun to grasp the diversity of the Canadian experience, past and present. Through a conscious program of citizenship education quite different from the conventional course in civics, they should have developed foundations of attitude and knowledge basic to participative citizenship in Canadian life locally, regionally, and nationally.

With this background, Canadian children will be ready for a more systematic study of the basic components of Canada Studies.

CHAPTER IV

Studying the Canadian Environment

A STRUCTURE FOR SECONDARY STUDIES

With foundations of citizenship education and initial understandings of the diversity of Canadian society developed in the elementary years, the first comprehensive study of Canada should be initiated as students enter secondary school. Because provinces of Canada do not organize their school systems in the same way, it is difficult to propose the exact grade or age level for this study. In provinces which divide the secondary years into junior and senior levels, this study should be during the junior years; in Quebec, it should be during the First Cycle of secondary school; in Ontario, it should be in those years identified as the Intermediate Level; in provinces where school levels are less sharply defined, it should be undertaken in the seventh or eighth year of schooling.

As indicated in Chapter 2, an understanding of Canada as a whole requires that the study of Canadian society must be seen as something more than the sum of many separate but related stories. Accordingly, an approach to the study of Canada which includes some history, some geography, some political science, some economics, and some sociology has demonstrated its weaknesses: Canada is examined consecutively from the perspectives of several different disciplines, but few students can at any time grasp a sense of the whole. Similarly, high school students who examine Canada through a series of thematic studies in multi-disciplinary fashion have experienced considerable difficulty because a reasonably full story of Canada requires not only the study of many themes but also the relationships among the themes. Further, students whose only study of Canada is through an "issues" course in senior high school commonly face the problem of attempting to study contemporary issues and questions without an adequate background of the nature and operation of Canadian society. Under these circumstances, only the most superficial and one-dimensional study of Canadian and world issues is possible.

Such current methods of studying Canada in the secondary schools reveal the need for an improved approach. Typically, histories of Canada have placed great emphasis on constitutional issues at the expense of other important dimensions of the Canadian story – quite apart from the almost universal phenomenon of never having the time to deal with those contemporary questions which are of most interest to students. Equally typically, very few Canadian high school students have the opportunity to study anything systematically about the Canadian economy, usually on the grounds that the discipline of economics is too complex (or too unfamiliar to Canadian teachers?). The study of Canadian politics is commonly included only as a subsection of Canadian History or Canadian Issues at senior levels and frequently is reduced to an arid analysis of structures of governments and organizational charts lest it become controversial or partisan.

One of the popular developments of the 1970s in several parts of Canada was the introduction of multicultural studies. In fact, however, multiculturalism courses frequently became a series of ethnic studies (or studies of the ethnic character of parts of Canada) which served to strengthen rather than balance the strong ethnocentric forces which have always prevailed in Canada. Furthermore, an emphasis on multicultural or ethnic studies has almost invariably distorted the importance of the ethnic character of Canada at the expense of equally important but less topical themes such as Canada's relations with the United States, regional economic disparities, or federal–provincial relations.

Without question, the single best example of lack of perspective in secondary school studies of Canada is the virtually nation-wide post-1970 preoccupation with the political survival of Canada in the face of the prospect of Quebec independence. For generations prior to 1970, English schools in most of Canada showed almost total indifference to the study of French Canadians within and beyond Quebec, except as a passing item of curiosity; similarly French schools, at least in Quebec, paid scant attention to the rest of Canada other than relations between Ottawa and Quebec governments. Shortly after the Péquiste election victory of 1976 and the numerous public calls for national unity, Quebec Studies in one form or another became popular in many English schools throughout Canada, while social studies in French Canada, and Quebec in particular, became even more insular as the rest of Canada was seen by Québecois teachers to be increasingly irrelevant if not foreign. Without minimizing the crucial nature of the national survival issue, it is clear that narrowing the focus of the study of Canada to the issues of national survival and French–English relations is a distortion of the Canada-as-a-whole reality to the disadvantage of equally significant questions in the eyes of many Canadians – Western alienation from central Canada, for example, or the future of the Far North, or the impact of the massive growth of government bureaucracies.

Given these and other inadequacies of fragmented or imbalanced approaches to the secondary school study of Canada and given the kind of elementary social studies curriculum proposed in Chapter 3, a basic curriculum question is: How should secondary school studies of Canada be organized to present a comprehensive picture of Canada and to avoid the imbalances which have resulted from disciplinary or thematic approaches?

Chapter 2 presented the argument that the integrity of Canada should be retained in all studies throughout the secondary years. For purposes of study, it was argued, Canadian society should first be viewed as a total environment; accordingly, the first secondary school course on Canada should be The Canadian Environment. Following an examination of the characteristics of this unique environment, students should have the opportunity to understand the essential characteristics of the systems Canada has developed to enable Canadian society to function in this environment. A second level of the secondary school study of Canada should therefore be The Canadian Political System and The Canadian Economic System. With an understanding of both environment and systems, Canadian students should then proceed to Canadian Public Issues, to which their understandings of the Canadian environment and the political and economic systems might be practically applied. This approach promises to overcome some of the major weaknesses of secondary school studies of Canada as they have been organized to date.

COMPONENTS OF THE CANADIAN ENVIRONMENT

It is proposed, then, that a course called The Canadian Environment be the formal starting point, after the elementary years, for a program of Canada Studies which will be extended over the entire span of the secondary school years. It is useful to recall at this point that the term *environment* is used here in a particular way, and in a broader sense than it is used in biology or ecology; it is used to refer to the composite of the physical, social, and cultural characteristics of Canada, viewed as a single entity. In general terms, the Canadian Environment course should focus on the basic features of Canada presented in Chapter 2, should examine these features in the contemporary setting but also in historical perspective, and should emphasize the interrelatedness of these features. Out of such a study should come a synthesis: a view of the nature of Canadian society seen as a whole, the consequence of a composite of the basic features of the Canadian environment and their interaction. The broad objective throughout the study should be to help students develop an overview of the character of Canadian society, the forces that have shaped it, and the institutions that have sustained it.

Accordingly, Canadian Environment may be thought of as having two major elements: the basic features of Canada themselves and particularly their interrelationships; and the consequences of the features and their interrelationships for Canadian society. Students should begin their study of the Canadian environment with an examination of the meaning of the first feature of Canadian society; as each succeeding feature is examined, it should be related to the students' understanding of previous features. Finally, after all features and their relationships have been examined, students should consider what the composite of these features and their interrelationships reveal about the character of Canada – what makes Canada unique and distinctive, just as every other political community is unique and distinctive.

WHAT SHOULD STUDENTS LEARN ABOUT CANADA?

1. Canada is a northern, vast, and regionally divided country.

One might begin the study of Canada's northern location, size, and divisions from any of several points, but it is particularly important not to assume that students already understand what these terms mean. A study of varieties of climatic conditions and vegetation within Canada might, for example, be a useful starting point for understanding* Canada's physical diversity, and out of such a study the significance of northernness, vastness, and regional division might well be developed or extended.

However, even more important than an understanding of the terms themselves is the understanding of the impact of these characteristics on the way of living of people in different parts of Canada. To understand the impact of the northernness of Canada, students should examine how differences in lifestyles between Yellowknife and Sarnia, for example, are prompted by climatic conditions. Equally, they might contrast life-styles in Canada with those in more temperate conditions as, for example, in the Caribbean or in Greece or in other societies with which they have some familiarity. Such studies should help students understand that where one lives influences how one lives, how one thinks, and what one values most highly.

Although understanding the northernness of Canada as a whole is the real point of emphasis, it would be worthwhile for students everywhere in Canada to give some attention at this point to the distinctiveness of life-styles, past and present, of the Far North, to compare them one to another, and to contrast them to characteristics of their own ways of living.

Viewed historically, the northern character of Canada is reinforced by an awareness that the North remains central in Canadian mythology even though few Canadians think consciously of it and even fewer live there – any more than most Americans live in the West or most Scots in the Highlands. Viewed in this fashion, the European origins of Canada begin not, as is often suggested, with Columbus and the explorers from southern Europe, but with the Vikings, Cabot, and Cartier, all of whom sailed from northern Europe. Their discoveries led to the development of the fur trade, an essentially northern enterprise, requiring trading posts, which can be thought of as the precursors of modern urban centres. The ultimate boundaries of this trade correspond remarkably with the boundaries of modern Canada; the international boundary accords, with the major exception of the Columbia, with the drainage divide that separates the

---

* Many sentences in this book begin with "Students should understand . . . ." Students cannot, of course, be expected to give measurable evidence of full mastery of each of these understandings. Rather, the statements of understandings are responses to the question: *What should students learn about Canada?* with the expectation that more complete understanding of each of these statements will develop with experience, with greater maturity, and with good teaching. These statements should be read as indicators of the direction good teaching should take. The degree, level, and quality of understandings that can reasonably be expected of different students is the legitimate domain of teachers, curriculum experts, and other specialists.

rivers draining into the northern oceans from those that drain southward; it also serves as a climatic divide that extends through a land mass where the climate is changing rapidly: Ottawa, only four hundred miles north of Cincinatti, is 16 degrees Celsius colder.

The geographic distinctiveness of Canada, based on its northern character, reflects the so-called Laurentian thesis of Canadian development which stresses Canada's historic integrity based on a vast trading system that extended eventually to the western Arctic and the Pacific coast. This historic unity was itself based on the geographic unity provided by the great east–west system of waterways beginning with the "Empire of the St. Lawrence." The Laurentian thesis as one hypothesis about Canadian development might be contrasted with other theses: those associated with continentalism (which sees Canada as a "natural" northward extension of a dominant North American physical and cultural milieu) and Marxism (which sees Canada as an exploited hinterland of imperialist powers – first France, then Great Britain, and now the United States).

Understanding the vastness of Canada involves far more than gross population figures or area measurements. The relative sparseness of the total population of Canada is of far less significance than the distribution of this population. Like its northern character, the size of Canada is not easily appreciated by most Canadians, who live in cities located in a narrow east–west population corridor adjacent to the United States. It is well known that 90 per cent of Canadians live within two hundred miles of the international boundary. Settled Canada resembles in shape a horizontal version of Chile. Beyond the populated zone lie the almost uninhabited territories that give Canada its vast size, appreciated only when it is realized that Victoria is as far west of St. John's as Warsaw is east and that Pelee Island on Lake Erie, our southernmost extent, is as far from the north coast of Ellesmere Island as it is from the Equator.

One impact of Canada's vastness is that many Canadians never get to know other Canadians or other parts of Canada, even within the east–west population corridor. Time, distance, and difficulties of travel have discouraged Canadians who live far apart from meeting frequently and understanding one another's concerns. Even the promotion of tourist travel in east–west directions has been difficult, in part because travel in southerly directions has been relatively simple and inexpensive, and in part because of the lure of more established cultures of Europe for eastern Canadians and the Far East for western Canadians.

Another impact of Canada's vastness is that Canada has considerably more living space than most other countries. Viewed historically, students should understand that size has made it very costly to build Canada "from sea to sea."

Students should understand that Canada is physically divided into distinct regions, one of the major sources of Canada's diversity. The identification of major physical regions (the Atlantic Region, the Great Lakes–St. Lawrence Lowlands, the Canadian Shield, the Far North, the Western Interior Lowlands, and the Pacific Cordilleran Region is one categorization of regions of Canada) should be the starting point. From there, students should examine the dominant characteristics of each region. The identification of physical differences within regions – particularly within the region in which the student lives – should be a lesser consideration.

The identification of the names of the provinces and territories of Canada and their capitals should not be a major concern at this stage; Canada's political subdivisions will be of greater significance in later studies of Canada's political systems, and a less formal introduction to them should have taken place in elementary grades.

Students should understand that, as a consequence of Canada's physical divisions, not all people in Canada have the same perspectives and interests; among other things, Canada is a society of strong regional interests and outlooks. Students should understand that physical barriers serve as social barriers and that people in each region have been substantially influenced by their physical surroundings. They should understand, for example, that the physical characteristics of the Far North, in contrast to those of southern coastal British Columbia, have meant that many British Columbians and northern Canadians have considerable differences in outlooks, customs, and values influenced by different physical settings. Viewed historically, they might appreciate the disaffection of Atlantic Canadians with central Canada as a result of a clash of two distinctive sets of economic priorities and preferences of life-styles.

In all, an examination of Canada's physical characteristics of size and regional differences should help students to understand that although in one sense Canada is one, in a physical sense Canada is at least six quite different units.

2. Canada has a broad natural resource base composed of both renewable and non-renewable resources.

Students should understand that, in comparison with most other countries of the world, Canada is rich in both renewable and non-renewable resources. In the initial study of Canada's resource base, emphasis should be given to the identification of areas where resources are located. The implications of resource use and depletion should be stressed rather than the memorization of amounts and names.

Students should also recognize that resources are culturally defined: that what is a resource depends upon the needs and wants, the attitudes and objectives, the levels of technology of people in a culture. Oil, for example, was not a resource to the indigenous peoples of Alberta; buffalo meat was. The transformation of the Canadian prairies from lands of low productivity to highly productive lands, utilizing soil once rated poorly, was largely the result of various mechanical inventions. The native people, however, looked with dismay at the ruthless European ploughing of the Dry Belt, foreseeing correctly that it would be very damaging to the soil.

Students should understand the differences between renewable and non-renewable resources, even though a more in-depth understanding will be developed in later studies of the Canadian economic system. They should see that many basic resources such as gas, oil, and minerals are indeed exhaustible and that, in consequence, the question of resource conservation has been, or should have been, a question of considerable concern to Canadians. At the same time, students should learn that exploitation of these resources has been a major means of acquiring the standard of living now taken for granted by many Canadians. They should also understand that the people to benefit most from the development of Canada's resources have not usually been the people of the region from which the resource was extracted; the benefits of resource development have more often gone to other Canadians or to people in other countries. A more detailed examination of the conservation–exploitation question may be deferred, but students should at least identify the issue at the beginning of secondary school.

Ideally, students should begin to develop a personal feel for the land of Canada, to recognize Canada's physical heritage as their legacy, the future of which rests with them. The development of this sense may be difficult for the many students who have only lived in a big city. In short, students need to identify with Canada's resources, including the people involved in exploiting them, and the processes by which exploitation and development occur. The resource-based, single-industry town has long been and remains a highly significant Canadian phenomenon; it is estimated that upward of six hundred such towns exist in Canada. Students should have opportunities to identify with this distinctive and pervasive aspect of the Canadian urban experience. Examination of the perilous position of Glace Bay or Sudbury or Kitimat or many other towns of Canada could well serve to illustrate the significance of resource development to Canadian standards of living.

In summary, students should understand that Canada is rich and diverse in resources, that resource extraction and development have improved the quality of life for many Canadians but not equally throughout Canada, and that Canada's resources must be nurtured wisely if they are to be of continuing benefit to Canadians and other more needy peoples of the world.

Having examined the first two basic features of Canada, students should then build relationships between them. They might observe, for example, that Canada's resource base is not evenly distributed and that, in consequence, some regions are more favored in terms of resources than others. Equally, they might explore the relationship between Canada's vastness and its resources base by noting how far most resources are from larger centres of development and population. The building of natural gas pipelines and the development of the tarsands of Alberta are topical examples of resources that are difficult and expensive to utilize – because Canada is a northern, vast, and regionally divided country.

3. Canada is an industrial, technological, and urbanized society.

In general terms, students should learn that Canada was once a predominantly rural society, that most parts of Canada have since become industrialized to the point where Canada is now recognized as having acquired the characteristics of any Western industrialized society, and that Canada is one of many societies that have entered the era of computers and space technology. They should examine Canada's evolution from a primary industry economic base, through the development of secondary manufacturing, to a major growth in recent years of the service or tertiary industries. A comparison of occupations of Canadians at various times in Canada's history would, for example, help us illustrate some consequences of industrial and technological development on the life-styles of most Canadians from coast to coast.

Students should understand that industrialization and technological development in Canada, as in other parts of the world, has been accompanied by a consistently increasing urbanization. Examination of the growth of towns, cities, and suburban areas and the corresponding decrease in rural living should establish the fact of increasing urbanization. Students should also consider some of the dominant reasons for this fact: broader job opportunities where industry and services have been established, transportation facilities between urban centres, social amenities and services available only where there are major concentrations of population.

Although students should later consider in some depth major consequences of industrialization, urbanization, and technological development, they should at this stage examine a variety of life-styles in Canada today: rural and urban, industrial and pre-industrial, technological and pre-technological. They should learn to assess advantages and disadvantages rather than develop hasty judgments about different patterns of living. Above all, they should be encouraged to establish relationships between how people live and what factors have prompted or required these life-styles.

Students might examine how burgeoning industrial growth required major social adjustments as Canada changed from a rural to an urban society. In 1880, for example, only one-fourth of Canadians lived in towns and cities; by 1920, half the population was urban and the actual number of city dwellers had multiplied by four. This resulted from a phenomenon observable in developing countries today: the drawing power of urban life and the desire to escape from a rural milieu that seems idyllic largely to those unfamiliar with it. Yet this growth also produced a sudden need to provide new services – transportation, sanitation, water supplies, public health, police and fire protection, among others – that most Canadians now take for granted.

The establishment of linkages among the three basic features of Canada examined to this point should be undertaken. Students should observe that the industrialization of Canada has been far more pronounced in the southern parts of Canada than in the north, that industrialization has been far from equal in different regions of Canada, that industrialization would not have been possible, at least at the pace at which it has taken place, without the extraction and utilization of resources, and that technological developments (especially in the fields of transportation and communications) have reduced problems associated with the vastness of Canada. They should understand that certain technologies (in the hydro-electric and pulp and paper fields, for example) have been particularly suited to Canada's resource base.

4. Canada is a culturally diverse, multi-ethnic country with two historically predominant linguistic and cultural groups.

A basic understanding of the development of the cultural composition of Canadian society and of its current ethnic and linguistic characteristics should be the broad objective on the study of this basic feature of Canada.

Students should understand that Innuit and Indian peoples were the original inhabitants of what is now called Canada, that their ways of living have been fundamentally different from those of Europeans who later came here, and that there is now controversy in Canada concerning their status as a result of this historical priority.

Students should appreciate that Canada's original peoples should not be viewed culturally as one, or even as two groups; on the contrary, they should understand that Innuit and Indians developed a variety of distinctive life-styles and values which have many common characteristics. Non-native students should learn about native life-styles, customs, and practices and should see them particularly in relation to the physical environments in which Canada's indigenous peoples have lived.

It is likely that most students in Canada at earlier age/grade levels will have studied some traditional Innuit and/or Indians; it is not important for students to study contemporary indigenous cultures to appreciate the difficulties these peoples have faced in trying to retain their preferred ways of living in the face of hostility, indifference, and arrogance of Canadians of European origin. Some consideration of current clashes of priorities and values between indigenous peoples and other Canadians should encourage a respect for Innuit and Indian cultural development and self-expression.

Students should understand that the Americas, and Canada in particular, were colonized by a number of European nations and that, as a result of this process, English and French have become the predominant linguistic and cultural groups of contemporary Canada. An examination of the historical relationships between French and English, and between these peoples and Indians, throughout Canada's history, should be directed primarily to the understanding that differences of culture, language, and values have been a persistent source of tension within Canada and pre-Canadian colonies. It is important to recognize that development of this major understanding does not require a detailed study of a long series of incidents of conflict.

Students should understand that, since the late eighteenth century, the English influence in Canada has been much more pronounced than that of the French and indigenous peoples, although not equally in all parts of Canada. They should see that commerce, industry, legal traditions, political institutions, and dominant social values within Canada have their roots primarily in British heritage. Students should come to appreciate that French-speaking Canadians have felt aggrieved, and particularly so on some occasions, because of English dominance in a society which their ancestors had colonized. They should understand that French and English Canadians have not had equal opportunities for cultural and economic self-fulfilment and self-expression. They should learn that this fact has consistently been a source of annoyance and frustration for French Canadians, and a source of misunderstanding and hostility for English Canadians.

Students do not need a systematic and detailed analysis of Canada's constitutional history. However, they should learn that English–French relations in Canada have been influenced by laws and constitutional arrangements which have acknowledged the existence of two major cultural groups in Canada and have attempted to regulate the relationships between these groups. They should see these laws and arrangements as human, imperfect, and changing efforts to solve real problems between very different groups within the same political community.

43

Students should not see English–French relations in Canada as solely an exercise in conflict and disagreement. They should see that, on an individual level, relations have frequently been excellent and mutually respectful; on a political level, there has been cooperation as well as disagreement; between groups there has been considerable constructive exchange. Nevertheless, students should not be shielded from the reality that English–French relations have been commonly characterized by discord and tension rather than mutual understanding; they should know that French Canadians have been proud of their distinctive heritage and concerned about its survival. They should understand that French Canadians have never considered themselves to be just another minority ethnic group in Canada. Equally, they should know that English Canadians have been proud of their distinctive heritage and have believed that their contributions have been beneficial to all Canadians. They should understand that English Canadians have never considered themselves to be oppressors.

Because French–English relations have been so central to any understanding of Canada's development, students should be encouraged to ask themselves: How would I, as a French Canadian, have reacted in this situation? How would I, as an English Canadian, have reacted in this circumstance? They should also ask: How would I, as an Innuit, have reacted to this event?

Students should see contemporary Canada as a multi-ethnic society. They should appreciate that there have been many non-French, non-English, non-indigenous peoples who have been in Canada for generations – and that they, like all others, have wanted to preserve much of their unique heritages while contributing to the general well-being of their new homeland. They should learn that large-scale immigration from virtually all parts of the world has been a late nineteenth- and twentieth-century development and that, as a result, the identification of Canadian cultures as English, French, and native has long been inappropriate and misleading. They should see this simplistic view as another legitimate source of tension among Canadians of different cultures and regions. They might, for purposes of vivid illustration, examine patterns of major waves of immigration and, in particular, the scale and diversity of immigration of the past thirty years.

Examination of Canada's cultural diversity and immigration patterns should not ignore the important phenomena of English-language immigration from the United States and other English-language countries, and recent French-language immigration from around the world. Students should learn that neither "English-speaking Canada" nor "French-speaking Canada" is one homogenous group but that both cultural and linguistic groups have important differences as well as common cultural characteristics. They should equally recognize that many Canadians do not identify themselves as English Canadians or French Canadians or indigenous peoples, but expect and deserve recognition as being as Canadian as anyone else in Canada.

To enrich understanding of the development of cultural diversity in Canada, students should become sensitive to difficulties encountered by people who move to a new land; they should examine problems of coping with a new language, being confronted with unfamiliar customs and practices, being regarded by others as strange and foreign, and trying to retain dignity in the face of discrimination.

French–English relations, multiculturalism, rights of indigenous peoples, and other cultural issues should each be seen as but one important dimension of a single basic feature of Canadian society. All dimensions of this feature need to be examined for a proper perspective on the cultural diversity of Canada. Furthermore, it should be reinforced that cultural diversity is only one feature of the total diversity of Canada.

After an examination of the several aspects of Canada's cultural composition, students should relate this basic feature of Canada to those previously studied. They might, for example, see that immigration has largely been confined to southern portions of Canada and that, as a result, tensions resulting from multi-ethnicity have not historically characterized the Far North, although conflicts of cultural values in the North have more recently been significant for all Canadians. Equally, they might observe the marked differences in cultural composition of the different regions of Canada and the uneven distribution of population, by ethnic origin, throughout Canada. In this context, students might appreciate why French–English relations and multiculturalism are quite different issues in Quebec from what they are in New Brunswick and Ontario, and even more different from what they are in Western Canada and the rest of the Atlantic provinces. They should begin to recognize why the encouragement of multiculturalism in Canada is viewed positively in the West and parts of Ontario, with anxiety in Quebec, and with greater detachment in much of Atlantic Canada.

Students might also examine if economic opportunity has been equally available to Canadians regardless of origin. They might examine problems of job opportunity for new arrivals in Canada. They might equally examine the extent to which new economic opportunities have opened up for Canadians from generation to generation.

Students might explore the relationship between urbanization and cultural diversity. They should learn that most Canadian urban centres are multicultural, that conflicts between cultural groups and outright discrimination toward people of a number of cultural groups has been a contemporary Canadian reality.

5. Canada is exposed to a multitude of external economic, political, and cultural influences.

The study of this basic feature of Canada should help students to understand that Canada is not, and never has been, a society in isolation; they should come to recognize that Canada has always been influenced by developments beyond its control and beyond its borders, has frequently influenced external events, and is very much a part of a complex, interrelated world community. Recent developments in Quebec have, for example, led to deliberate efforts to cultivate Canada's association with francophone countries throughout the world as an expression of our francophone character. Historic ties with the United Kingdom developed from membership in the Commonwealth to special associations with Caribbean, African, and Asian nations. Economic and other relations with Japan, China, the Soviet Union, Western Europe, and Latin America foster an outward view that should serve as a healthy antidote to an exclusive preoccupation with things Canadian.

Students should see that Canadian life has been dramatically shaped by British and European factors and that, in turn, Canada has adapted great variety of externals to the Canadian setting. A study of Canada's colonial heritage should provide vivid testimony to Canada's exposure to a considerable number of political, economic, and cultural influences. Students will later study the origins of Canada's political traditions; at this stage, an examination of artistic influences could be very revealing.

One aspect of Canada's exposure deserves special attention: exposure to the United States. It is remarkable that, despite vastness, Canada has but one land neighbor, forcing a turn to the oceans for links with other nations. Almost inevitably, the United States has served as a reference point for Canadians; indeed, it has been argued that Canada's situation in North America has caused Canadians to direct many of their negative feelings about all other nations toward a single country because Canada does not have contiguous boundaries with any other nations. It is also worth observing that two such large societies have had contiguous economic and population cores; if, as once seemed possible, New Orleans rather than New York had become the great American metropolis, Canadian (and American) history would have been quite different. The contemporary susceptibility of Canadians to American influences (for example, television and the cultural values it espouses) is the most obvious example. The existence and impact of U.S.-based international corporations in the Canadian economy are also understandable aspects of exposure, in this case of an economic nature. Similarly, the fact that Canada has been an active participant in major defence agreements with the United States should illustrate the special impact of exposure to and influence by the United States.

Students should do at least a preliminary analysis of costs and benefits of being a member of a world community. Although detailed examination of the history of foreign investment in Canada is not appropriate here, students should recognize that many of the economic benefits Canadians currently enjoy would not have been possible without foreign investment. A systematic examination of British colonial history is not required; students should nevertheless recognize the strong influence of Britain on Canada's commercial life and political values, among other things. A comprehensive review of the French regime in Canada is not necessary for a basic understanding of the impact of the clergy on life in New France. A study of European immigration to Western Canada provides the opportunity to see how a variety of peoples have helped to shape the character of contemporary Canada.

Most recent world developments provide many contemporary examples of Canada's interdependence. Canada has always been a trading nation, but is now particularly vulnerable to world market influences. Canada's production for export has usually found ready markets; it now faced much stiffer competition not only from its older competitors but also from newly developing nations of the world. The ability of Canada to compete in international commerce is significantly influenced by labor costs and productivity within Canada. Canadian producers face tougher competition from imported goods, and the protection of Canadian markets for domestic producers has been a perennnial issue.

Canada's exposed character has never been more fully demonstrated than by her participation in the two world wars. Examination of this participation can throw much light on Canada's developing international role, international relationships, and their connection to Canada's own development as a nation. Economically and politically, both wars contributed to a growing national maturity – and to internal tensions; they demonstrated Canada's vulnerability to external events and policies over which Canada had little influence.

Students should also recognize that Canadians have made important international contributions even though Canada has never been a major world power. Canada's stance at times of international crisis, the international recognition of Canadian artists and scholars and scientists, Canada's peacekeeping roles, and Canada's participation in world organizations can serve to illustrate Canadian influence in the world community. Although Canada may face its own identity crisis, there is little doubt on the world scene about the reality of Canada.

Building relationships between this basic feature of Canada and those previously studied should provide little difficulty. Canada's northern character is shared with several nations of the world and provides a basis for contrast with others. Canada's resource utilization is a matter of international as well as national significance. Canada's industrial and technological status is very much related to Canada's international economic role. Canada's ability to deal effectively with internal tensions between regions and cultural groups is of genuine concern to Canada's international partners. Canada's multicultural character does much to explain why Canadian foreign policy has always been a matter of controversy in times of international crisis.

ILLUSTRATING RELATIONSHIPS AMONG BASIC FEATURES

Once all of the basic features of Canada have been examined and initial relationships established among them as suggested above, it would be valuable for students to analyse contemporary issues which illustrate a whole variety of relationships. One such issue might be the building of a pipeline from the Far North. This issue could be examined in such a way as to help students not only understand the debate itself but also develop skills in building relationships. It should not be expected that teachers teach this example; rather, the example is presented to illustrate a range of possible relationships that might be considered in the study of any major topical issue.

Any discussion of a pipeline immediately draws attention to Canada's natural resource base – the location and reserves of oil and gas and the existence of other energy sources such as uranium, coal, and hydro-electric power. The Arctic location of so much of Canada's oil and gas reserves raises questions of the delicately balanced ecology of the Far North and the consequent concerns about protecting the physical environment. The fact that Canada is an industrialized country will bring up considerations of the various technologies that place demands on the country's energy supplies. The sheer size of the country and its resulting transport needs, its unique geographic position and long cold winters, the concentration of its population in a few large cities, certain life-styles such as winter holidays in the sun or the weekend trek to the cottage or the proliferation of recreational vehicles and power boats, all give vivid meaning to the bald fact that Canadians are the largest per capita users of oil and gas in the world.

By consciously directing attention to the basic features of Canada, teachers can reinforce the relationships involving the exposure of Canadian society to the United States, the energy needs and policies of the United States and those of Canada – questions that are interrelated still further by the dominance of the Canadian petroleum industry by a few, mainly American-based, oil companies. The capital costs of such a vast project as a pipeline indicate that Canadians might have to find external sources of capital for construction and certainly would have to borrow very substantially. In addition, American concerns about an all-Canadian route have led to suggestions that they develop their own alternative route, involving huge tankers moving through the coastal waters of British Columbia. These are only some of the relationships that might be demonstrated.

The uneven distribution of natural resources in such a large country as Canada complicates all efforts to establish Canadian energy policies. Some provinces have no oil or gas and must rely on offshore, more costly sources; others, such as heavily industrialized Ontario, are dependent on domestic supplies from Alberta and Saskatchewan. An incident like the pipeline debate, therefore, raises many questions associated with regional disparities, economic concentrations, rivalries within Canada for new petrochemical and refining industries, and others arising from the basic nature of Canadian society.

The debate also provides opportunities to understand other aspects of Canadian society. The appointment of a commission to examine the issue of a northern pipeline and make recommendations, the flood of submissions and briefs by native peoples, environmentalists, rival oil and gas companies, central Canadian industrialists, as many other concerned groups; the pressures exerted on government by these same groups; the diplomatic negotiations between Ottawa and the provinces as well as Washington: all these facts should introduce students to some of the difficulties of major decision-making in Canada.

A decision to build a pipeline from the Far North involves altering the Canadian environment in many ways and for generations to come. Depending on the type of decision, it could conflict with land claims of native peoples; it could result in major shifts in the location of industry and population; it could substantially influence the life-styles of native peoples and many other Canadians; it will partly determine how long Canada's supplies for oil and gas will last; it will have long-term effects on Canada's balance of international payments and thus on the entire Canadian economy; and it will certainly become a factor in all future Canadian–American relations. These are some illustrations of ways in which the factors in a decision about a major public issue relate directly to the very nature of Canadian society and its interacting basic features.

CONSEQUENCES FOR CANADIAN SOCIETY

As noted earlier in the chapter, there is a second element to a study of the Canadian environment: an examination of the consequences of these basic features and their interrelationships for Canadian society. Students, then, should have the opportunity to synthesize by examining the following questions: What do these features and their interrelationships, looked at together, tell us about the character of Canada? What is unique or particular about Canada as a political community? What distinguishes Canada from other political communities of the world?

Students should quickly recognize that the individual basic features of Canada are not unique. Other nations have a northern location; others are regionally divided; many are multicultural; many are industrialized; all are exposed. But they should also recognize that no other political community has the same composite of basic features and the same relationships among them. And that is what makes Canada a unique political community; just as all other political communities have a unique composite of basic features and particular relationships among them.

By way of synthesis, there are more specific understandings about the particular character of Canadian society that should develop from a study of the Canadian environment. Students should see that all people in Canada have fundamentally similar needs and wants: adequate food, clothing, shelter; the rights to free expression and free association; opportunity to be usefully employed and to have joyful leisure; freedom to worship (or not worship) as they see fit; equality before the law; dignity and human respect; and the opportunity to be themselves.

They should at the same time recognize that, largely as a result of the particular characteristics of Canadian society, Canadians tend to think of themselves as members of groups, not only as individuals and as Canadians; that Canadians tend to identify themselves at one and the same time as Prince Edward Islanders, Atlantic Canadians, unionists, members of the United Church, members of a social organization, and Canadians. They should begin to note that each sub-group regards itself as somewhat different from other groups in terms of interests, aspirations, and priorities. They should recognize that each group legitimately wishes to express itself and to satisfy its interests in the ways that it prefers. They should begin to understand that most Canadians, because of their group affiliations, are people of multiple loyalties. They should begin to appreciate that Canada as a whole has only a limited claim on the loyalty of Canadians, and that many kinds of other loyalties can be fully compatible with a common loyalty to the one political community.

Students should recognize that loyalties are not only multiple but frequently in conflict. They should see, for example, that ethnic loyalties have been opposed to economic loyalties, that rural values are frequently in conflict with the dominant values of the region in which one lives, that the priorities of conservationists are very different from those of land developers, even when all speak the same language. They should see that a person can at one and the same time be of Swedish origin, live in Alberta, be a member of the Social Credit party, a Methodist, an operator of a small family business, a Westerner, and a Canadian – and that all these loyalties can exist side by side.

Students should learn that the diversity within Canadian society has been reinforced by a variety of events since Confederation. They should note the almost total absence of extended periods of stability or tranquillity. Recurring injections of new population, and a sequence of turbulent periods or events (the Post-Confederation period, World War One, the Great Depression, World War

Two, the pace of contemporary social change resulting from technological developments) can be identified; such developments may well have diverted Canadian energies away from activities and developments which might otherwise have encouraged greater internal harmony. Time and circumstance may not have provided Canada with the breathing room necessary to develop the degree of social cohesion necessary for the development of mutual understanding and respect among diverse peoples in any society.

Students should see that Canadians have established numerous organizations which encourage them to express their distinctiveness and to reinforce their group loyalties. An examination of the origins and objectives of a variety of these institutions, both familiar and unfamiliar to the students, should illustrate this understanding. Community centres, consumer groups, historical societies, cultural clubs, churches, service organizations, and fraternal societies are some social institutions whose study could be revealing.

Students should understand that the strong group identities in Canada, as elsewhere, have made mutually satisfactory decision-making for all groups complex and difficult. They should see Canadian diversity as a continuing challenge to all Canadians – a challenge to achieve an appropriate balance of diversity and commonality.

Students should begin to recognize that, if Canada is to respond to the legitimate and diverse aspirations of all its members, some level of consensus among Canadians is necessary to balance the normal frictions among groups in Canada. They might begin to consider what level of consensus within Canadian society is desirable to respect the diversity of Canada, the reality that Canada is part of an interdependent world and the need to respond equally to the needs and expectations of all Canadians. This exploration can lead students to see Canada's problems in a broader perspective and to view themselves and Canada in relation to the problems facing peoples in other parts of the world. Such a study can lead to a greater sensitivity to the difficulties which have faced all leaders in Canada and to a consideration of goals that might be pursued by all Canadians regardless of their diversity of interests, values, and priorities.

THE NEXT STEP

Two major strands of study should now have been developed through the elementary years and the beginning of secondary school. First, students should have developed initial understandings of the complexity of Canada through a study of different Canadian communities in the elementary grades, followed by a study of the whole environment of Canada in the first years of secondary school. Secondly, they should have developed a growing awareness of the tasks citizens must assume and the challenges which are presented to the people of Canada if their society is to operate as a cohesive political community in the best interests of all. These two strands form the basis for a civic education appropriate to Canadian society.

With this basis of understanding of *what* Canada is, it is now desirable to examine *how* Canada functions, to examine the systems Canada has developed and adapted to the environment. The study of the Canadian environment has

50

provided the setting; study of Canada's political and economic systems, which should now follow in the middle years of secondary school, will help students to understand Canadian institutions and processes in action.

CHAPTER V

Studying the Canadian Political System

The Canadian political system can be regarded as a product of the five basic features of Canada and the kind of society that has evolved as the result of the interactions between them. An understanding of our federal system of government is to be found not only in the legal and constitutional arrangements between the various levels of government but also in the diverse forces – geographic, economic, social, cultural – that have made the formal structures of federalism necessary The essence of federalism is not in the institutional or constitutional structure but in society itself. Federal government is a political device by which the federal qualities of society are expressed and protected.

Until recently, students of federalism were concerned primarily with formal structures, constitutional niceties, division of powers, amending procedures, constitutional law, and so on. Some knowledge of the institutional structures and constitutional arrangements between the two main levels of government is necessary; however, the major purpose of this chapter is to emphasize the political culture and the social realities that breathe life into Canadian federalism, that determine how it actually works, that generate problems and create stress, and that require constant readjustment of the informal procedures between the provinces and the central government.

There has been some tendency to picture parliamentary democracy in Canada as an ideal system where legislative power resides in an elected parliament, where the Prime Minister and cabinet are responsible to the elected majority and where, therefore, ultimate power lies in the hands of the people. Such an ideal system, even assuming it ever did exist, has been dramatically altered by the impact of several factors; any realistic approach to the study of Canada's political system must deal with these factors.

The study also should emphasize the vital importance of support for the political community as a whole and the system by which it is governed. Students should understand that Canada, like any other political community, requires a high level of support from its members if it is to survive in some viable form. Its members must in turn perceive Canada as a community in which their needs are basically satisfied. Support for the Canadian political community and its system of government, however, should not be confused with support for those who are in control of the system at any given time; the latter, although they spend energy and money trying to ensure their own continuing positions, are expendable, and democratic techniques exist for their legitimate removal when they fail to satisfy their clients.

For whatever reasons, there is strong evidence to indicate that far too many students leave school without having studied Canada's political system and, not surprisingly, have virtually no idea of the structure of the system or how it works. There is also evidence to indicate that young people are becoming increasingly cynical about politics, and that schools, as one of the agents of political socialization are, by default, partly responsible. A democratic society that tolerates such a situation for long takes unwarranted risks with its own stability, and does a disservice to students whose lives will be so pervasively influenced by governments and the total political system.

A study of the Canadian political system which develops from an understanding of the character of the Canadian environment and the basic features that help shape it, and which emphasizes the network of relationships between the system and the environment, is one which should encourage pan-Canadian understanding and active, informed citizenship.

This chapter is directed exclusively to the question: What should young Canadians *understand* about the political system of their own country? No attempt is made to describe the detailed information that students will need to reach any of the understandings. It is assumed that teachers, using the set of questions and the understandings in the following pages as guidelines, will be able to readily identify the kinds of information required for classroom use.

The questions are intended for use by teachers. They were desgined on the assumption that teachers who are familiar with the literature in this area can identify the significance of the questions and reword them for practical classroom purposes without difficulty.

The understandings and the information on which they are based should not be presented as closed systems of knowledge with all the answers predetermined. For students starting from scratch, it is desirable to create a spirit of inquiry in the classroom by designing open-ended questions that will lead students to the evidence and enable them to reach their own conclusions. With the guidance of good teachers, the majority of students should arrive at reasoned and defensible understandings based on adequate information.

The understandings should be regarded not as rigid prescriptions for all students but as comprehensive guidelines to be modified by teachers to suit the backgrounds, capabilities, and limitations of their own students.

UNDERSTANDING THE CANADIAN POLITICAL SYSTEM

A. CONTEMPORARY ANALYSIS

1. The structure of Canadian society

What is meant by the phrase "the federal structure of Canadian society"?

To what extent is the federal structure of our society determined by the basic features of Canada?

a) Students should understand that federal societies are very diverse and complex; they are composed of groups each of which regards itself as different from the others, having different values, attitudes, expectations, and backgrounds that all require opportunities for self-expression.

b) Students should understand that each of the basic features of Canada has helped create the diversities and complexities of Canadian society. In other words, they should understand that the federal structure of our society is primarily caused by the basic features of the country and the interactions between them.

c) Students should understand that very few wholly integrated societies exist; most are characterized in varying degrees by diversities, yet not all of them can be described as federal states. Thus students should understand what particular aspects of the basic features of Canada justify classifying ours as a federally structured society.

d) Students should have some understanding of the nature of tension and the fact that diversities inevitably cause certain kinds of stress. In particular, students should understand that tension, controversy, and conflict of viewpoints are not only inevitable in all societies, they are also, within broad limits, desirable. Many examples are available to illustrate that the resolution of conflict and the lessening of tension between competing groups in Canada have had beneficial results. On the other hand, it is important for students to understand that under certain circumstances tension levels can become dangerously high. When this happens, tensions are no longer constructive and may become detrimental or destructive. Again, examples are available to illustrate this understanding.

e) Students should begin to understand some of the qualities that its citizens must possess if a federally structured society is to survive in a healthy and vigorous condition. They might also consider whether Canadians have these qualities and, if not, how they might be developed.

2. Canada's federal system of government

What is a federal system of government?

Considering the basic features of the country, to what extent does a federal system of government seem to be appropriate for Canada?

What are the strengths and weaknesses of a federal system of government and how are these revealed in Canada?

a) Students should become familiar with the term political community. They should understand that, unlike expressions such as nation, state, nation-state that do have value connotations in the minds of many people and are subject to differing interpretations, a political community is a value-free term used simply to describe any group of people living within clearly defined, generally recognized boundaries, having a system of government and other shared institutions. Students should understand that the political community called Canada is only one form of human association and that it is composed of many other kinds of communities or groups based on family, neighborhood, region, ethnic origin, religion, language, economic status, and other factors.

b) Students should understand that the federal structure of Canadian society requires a government that will accommodate the country's diversities within some form of central framework. Students should understand that, although there are other alternatives, the Canadian federal system consists of a central government, ten provincial governments, and a great number of municipal governments.

c) Students should understand that a federal system of government requires some kind of written agreement to divide powers between the two main levels of government and that, in Canada, this is provided primarily in certain sections of the British North America Act. Students should know enough about the division of powers between the federal and provincial governments to understand that the division reflects some of the most important aspects of the federal structure of Canadian society.

d) With their knowledge of the federal structure of Canadian society and government, students should understand why intergovernmental disputes occur. They should begin to understand that Canada's political system is a delicately balanced federation continually faced with the problems of finding acceptable national goals while at the same time trying to meet the aspirations of all its diverse groups and parts.

e) Building on their studies of tension and its causes, students should understand that the Canadian political community to which they belong requires a minimum ability among its members to resolve conflict with tolerance, knowledge, and understanding of opposing viewpoints. With this ability, it may be possible for the federal government, in cooperation with the provinces, to continue to balance contending interests, to resolve recurring conflicts, to maintain acceptable levels of tension, to provide sufficient satisfactions to the majority of its citizens, and thus to sustain the Canadian political community in some viable form.

On the other hand, students should understand that if social cleavages become too deep, if the legitimate aspirations of any large cohesive group or region are not met, or if they conclude they can do better on their own, or if the quality of life is no longer satisfactory to the majority, then it will become increasingly difficult to maintain the political community called Canada.

3. Political values, attitudes, and behavior of Canadians

What is meant by the terms political values, political attitudes, and political behavior?

What are the most obvious political values and attitudes held by Canadians and by what forces (for example, family, church, peer group, school, place of residence, sex, social status) are they formed? In particular, how do the basic features of the country influence the political values and attitudes of people in Canada?

56

What kinds of political behavior are exhibited by Canadians as a result of their values and attitudes? To what extent are these kinds of behavior beneficial or detrimental to the Canadian political community?

In what ways do political values, attitudes, and behavior of Canadians vary in different parts of the country and to what extent are these variations caused by the basic features of Canada?

What changes in the political values, attitudes, and behavior of Canadians might enhance Canada as a political community and how might these changes be brought about?

a) Students should understand that political behavior is a term used to describe activities associated with any aspect of the political system; it includes such things as voting, belonging to a political party, taking part in an election campaign, participating in a demonstration for or against some public issue, being a member of an interest group trying to influence government, and so on. The political behavior of Canadians is determined by their attitudes toward politics; that is, by the beliefs and feelings they have toward the political community as a whole, its system of government, and the authorities in control of the system at any given time.

Students should understand that social scientists have begun to use public surveys and other research techniques to gather a great amount of detailed information about political attitudes and behavior of Canadians. Most of this research will be rather pointless unless the questions "Why?" and "What difference does it make?" are frequently asked. For example, research evidence suggests that very young voters, no matter where they live or what they do for a living, are less likely to be politically active than those in the middle-age bracket. Unless convincing answers can be found for the preceding two questions, this piece of information about the age profile of Canadian voters will leave most students totally unimpressed.

Students should understand the difference between political values and attitudes. Attitudes are more specific and are directed toward political parties, politicians, current issues, and day-to-day operations of the system. Values are deep-seated, fundamental principles providing the very foundations of a political community.

b) Among the political values that Canadian students should understand are the following: the inherent worth of individual personality; the basic freedoms of speech, assembly, association, and conscience; the rule of law and equality before the law regardless of religion, ethnic origin, economic status, or other factors; political equality, the principle of one man, one vote, and the right to choose between alternatives; popular sovereignty and the right of all citizens to participate in selecting and controlling their government; the acceptance of majority rule in the election of individual candidates and in the decision-making processes of government; the recognition that the majority does not have absolute power nor the right to ride rough-shod over its opponents, that it must consider the wishes of the minority, and attempt to govern in the interests of as many people as possible.

57

Students might investigate a few cases where groups of Canadians seem to have pursued their objectives by undemocratic means and ask such questions as: Why did the group behave as it did? Were its members so convinced of their own righteousness that they felt they could trample on the rights of others? Were they retaliating against people who also had resorted to undemocratic tactics? Did they not understand the principles of democracy or did they feel so keenly or frustrated that they did not care? Were the means used by the group justified by the end results? Are such cases increasing in Canada and if so, why? What effect does the employment of undemocratic methods have on the political community as a whole? What democratic ideals appear to be violated most frequently? Do these cases indicate that the ideals of democracy are not as deeply ingrained in our society as is commonly assumed? How does Canada compare in these respects to other political communities? Students might also consider the much more difficult question of whether a province or a cohesive group has the right to secede from the Canadian political community and what strategies are available for this purpose.

Students should understand that the political values listed previously are also held by the people of many other democratic countries. This raises the question of whether or not there are any uniquely Canadian political values. Although social scientists are still debating some aspects of this question, there appears to be agreement that, compared to people from many other countries, Canadians are not as interested in politics, are more traditional and cautious, are less ruggedly individualistic and more content to work for group goals, are more deferential to leadership and willing to let the government do things for them, and seem to be less volatile and not as prone to violence. Students should understand that generalities of this kind can be misleading, that they are stated as comparisons with some other countries and not as absolutes, that they may be part of Canada's mythology or that they may describe a political culture that existed in the past.

c) Students should understand that political attitudes are elusive, subject to many variables, and relate to almost all aspects of the political system and its operations. Attitudes toward political parties, election campaigns, public issues, the efficiency or honesty of governments, party leaders, local candidates, and so on can vary depending on age, occupation, sex, education, ethnicity, rural, urban and regional place of residence, religion, language, and other factors.

Social scientists have produced a growing amount of statistical evidence and analyses about political attitudes. How much of all this data should be investigated in the schools must be left to the discretion of individual teachers. However, there are some generalities that students should understand, the most significant probably being the tremendous regional diversity of political attitudes in this country. Canada has several political cultures, with a wide boundary line down the Ottawa River. Some analysts have argued that, compared to the rest of Canada, the Atlantic provinces and Quebec are less progressive, less confident about the future, more intolerant of ethnic minorities and other religious groups, more authoritarian and in favor of law and order, much more politically cynical and disinterested, and more convinced that, as individuals, they have little power to influence governments. On the other hand, British Columbia, closely followed

58

by Ontario, appears to be the most highly politicized, with the Prairie provinces somewhere in between. Compared to other Canadians, the people in British Columbia and Ontario have been portrayed as being more interested in politics, more certain of their own political power, more confident about the future, less cynical about governments, and less intolerant of various minority groups.

Students should understand that political attitudes naturally help to determine voting behavior. There is evidence to suggest that people with similar attitudes tend to support the same political party. Students should examine some of this evidence in order to understand what groups traditionally support each of the major parties and why they do so. What party seems to have the most appeal for urban middle-class voters, for recent immigrants, for well-educated people, for French-speaking Canadians, for prairie farmers or for the working class? An analysis of questions like this should help students to understand the importance of attitudes in determining party affiliations and voting patterns and thus give them additional insights into the functioning of the Canadian political community.

Although every election campaign is different, students should understand that Canadians have a number of general attitudes that will affect their vote on certain issues in almost all elections. It could be argued, for instance, that regional economic disparities should be a concern for all Canadians and yet the evidence from a number of election campaigns reveals that most of those who live in prosperous areas really don't care about the economic difficulties faced by Canadians in depressed regions. Students might consider whether this apparently selfish, thoughtless, or uninformed attitude is injurious in a political community like Canada. The evidence also suggests that the majority of Canadians are primarily concerned with immediate bread-and-butter issues and are indifferent to long-term questions such as resource use and conservation, the prospects for nuclear proliferation, or relations with the Third World. In other words, the political attitudes of Canadians tend to be short-sighted and egocentric.

This may be explained or excused, in part, by the attitude Canadians have about their own political power. Numerous opinion surveys clearly indicate the majority of people believe that, as individuals, they have very little political power. The feeling that the government is big, remote, and too complex for comprehension and that the individual, therefore, does not have much influence is prevalent in all parts of the country and in all socio-economic groups, although it is most frequently found, as might be expected, in less prosperous areas and among those near or below the poverty line.

Naturally, if people believe they have little influence they will not participate actively in either party politics or the electoral process nor are they likely to be interested in long-term policy questions. While three out of every four Canadians usually vote in federal elections – the percentage is much smaller in many provincial and almost all municipal elections – they are only mildly interested in party politics the rest of the time. If the contest is a good one and especially if it involves colorful personalities, most Canadians will follow an election campaign closely and will turn out at the polls, but this is about the extent of their political activity. It has been said that Canadians participate in the whole electoral process like interested spectators at a hockey game.

59

Students should understand that this type of behavior has some important consequences for the political system. Because the candidates and the minority who are really active in party politics are mainly from well-educated middle- or upper-class backgrounds, the government is in the hands of people who are fairly satisfied with the status quo. Conversely, a great many Canadians, particularly those who might gain from change, sit on the sidelines, exerting little influence over government yet being subject to a multitude of its decisions. Furthermore, the apparent lack of any real interest in the day-to-day operations of the government allows the political leaders, the senior civil servants, and the heads of major interest groups – the so-called elites – to work out compromises and make decisions without having to worry too much about the general public.

d) In general terms, students should understand how political attitudes are formed and what the more significant agents of political socialization are. They should understand that attitudes are formed subconsciously, and that almost every aspect of social life may influence attitude formation. Political attitudes begin to develop early in life mainly through the influence of family, school, peer group, and the media.

The family is probably the most important of these four. The relationships within the family, the father's occupation, the table-talk that goes on, all have an influence. Obviously, if the father is, say, a shop steward keenly interested in union activities and inclined to unburden himself at home, his children will pick up either by acceptance or rejection some political attitudes. Although the school is also very influential, the results of formal instruction are unpredictable and frequently the opposite to what the teacher hoped. A lesson may be designed to develop feelings of tolerance or an interest in party politics, but if the teacher is authoritarian or the discussion is dull, the desired results may not be achieved. The general atmosphere of a school, the spirit with which it is administered and especially the activities in the playgrounds are probably more influential in attitude formation than is the classroom. What students read in out-of-school time and what they watch on television or at the movies have strong effects on the development of attitudes.

Students should understand that youthful political attitudes which tend to be idealistic, positive, and supportive are formed before young Canadians have any opportunity to participate in the political system. Their attitudes, therefore, are likely to change once they have direct experience with it. Although the early influences may persist, the predominant factor in adult life probably will be membership in one or more of the interest groups that are considered in detail in a later section. At this point, students should understand only that members of a group formed for economic or other purposes tend to develop similar attitudes and that over 60 per cent of all Canadians do belong to one or more organizations having some political interests.

Finally, students should understand that the basic features of Canada and the resulting federal structure of society are not only very important factors in the development of attitudes but are also the "objects" toward which political attitudes are directed. It is recommended that each of the basic features of the country should be analysed from this perspective. For example, the exposure of

60

Canada to American economic and cultural influences certainly affects the formation of political attitudes in this country; conversely, some of these attitudes are directed toward American-based multinational corporations, American professors in Canadian universities, and so on. Above all, students should keep in mind that Canada is a regionally divided country, that the majority of French Canadians, one of our two founding races, are concentrated in one province, and that some of the most important political attitudes of Canadians are not only regionally based but are also sometimes directed toward other regions.

4. The party system and the electoral process in Canada

What are political parties, and what functions are they intended to perform in a parliamentary democracy like Canada?

In what ways do the basic features of Canada influence the structure, kinds of leadership, policies, and strategies of national political parties in Canada? As a result, how effectively do political parties carry out their various functions in Canada?

What are the most important features of the electoral system in Canada? What evidence exists to indicate whether party politics and federal general elections are divisive or unifying influences in Canada?

a) Students should understand that a political party is an organization formed primarily to win elections; that in Canada, winning means getting more members elected to the House of Commons (or a provincial legislature) than any other party, that an election victory gives a political party the right to form a government; that in a parliamentary democracy, this means the leader of the victorious party becomes prime minister and that he selects his cabinet from among his followers in the House of Commons. Therefore, since elections may be regarded in part as a technique for selecting the country's political decision-makers, the quality of a party's top men and women should be an important consideration for voters.

Students should understand that the Liberal party and the Progressive Conservative party, sometimes called the old-line parties, have been in existence continuously for a long period of time; that as society has become more complex and for other reasons, these parties seemed incapable of satisfying all the diverse interests of Canadians so that newer, third parties have developed at both the federal and provincial levels of government. They should understand, therefore, that the party system in Canada frequently involves the rivalry of more than two parties and that this increases the prospects of a minority government in which no one party has a clear majority of seats in the House of Commons (or a provincial legislature). The merits of minority government is a debatable point that students might consider.

Students should understand that for election purposes, Canada (and any province) is divided into districts called constituencies or ridings and that each district returns only one member to the House of Commons. Through simple studies of specific elections, students should understand that the Canadian electoral process can produce distorted results in which the number of seats won by the contending parties does not reflect their percentage of the popular vote. In other words, it is quite possible for a party to win a large majority of seats and form a government with only minority support from the total Canadian electorate. Conversely, a party may have a substantial percentage of the popular vote and yet win a disproportionately small number of seats.

b) Students should understand that in order to contest elections political parties need some kind of permanent organization. Although this varies from one party to another, all have officers (usually unpaid) who are elected for a fixed period of time in separate riding, provincial, and national meetings of the party faithful; these officers are assisted at the provincial and federal levels by small staffs of permanent, salaried employees.

In between elections the party organization tends to be flimsy, not particularly active, and frequently in debt. During the two months or so preceding a general election, the party apparatus springs to life, literally thousands of Canadians volunteer to work for the party of their choice, advertising and other public relations experts are hired, campaign managers are appointed at all levels, and office staffs are greatly expanded. When the election is over, the party organization tends to shrivel up again, leaving only the small permanent staffs, the elected officers and the winning candidates; of these three groups the most visible and important are the members of Parliament.

From their previous studies of the activities of political parties during a campaign, students should understand that elections cost a lot of money, that the amount spent by individual candidates and parties varies considerably, and that party funds must be raised primarily from private sources. They should understand that this method of financing political parties is open to abuse; donors to a campaign fund may expect and sometimes get favors in return, although such favors are not as frequently given or as flagrant as is often assumed. A number of important reforms introduced in 1974 were designed to reduce the abuses of campaign financing.

c) Students should understand that, in order to appeal to as many voters as possible, political parties must evaluate the interests of organized groups in society and try to produce a statement of policy called a party platform to attract such groups. Considering the size of the country and the great diversity of interests, it is understandable that successful parties design platforms which are stated in general, usually ambiguous, terms and all tend to sound alike. Students should understand that this may be one of the reasons why in federal and most provincial elections, issues are usually glossed over and the emphasis is placed on personalities and leadership. Thus all parties will promise in the campaigns to cut down unemployment, maintain full production, reduce taxes and yet increase government services and so on, without any indication exactly how these things will be achieved.

Nevertheless, students should understand that all parties reveal general tendencies differentiating one from another. All parties pour out information about issues and government actions for anyone who wants it; they do offer choices to the voters; they usually make democratic politics visible and interesting during an election campaign; and they do, therefore, perform many important functions

62

as a by-product of trying to win control of the governments. Thus, students should understand that, as members of the political community, it is important for them to identify the basic differences between political parties in Canada.

d) Students should understand that the basic features of the country are important factors in any consideration of political parties and the electoral process. Although the structure of party organizations, the look-alike nature of their platforms, the persistence of certain voting patterns, the sources of campaign funds, and other aspects of party politics and elections are in part products of the federal structure of Canadian society that might be considered, the critical question here is as follows: Do party politics, election campaigns, and the single-member plurality system of deciding results serve as unifying influences or do they strengthen regional differences and social cleavages? .

While recognizing that a highly centralized system of government is neither possible nor desirable in Canada, students will understand by this time that a country having a federally structured society requires institutions and techniques to bridge regional, cultural, linguistic, ethnic, and economic cleavages and encourage national understanding between all its diverse elements. It has been generally assumed that national political parties do counterbalance divisive forces by putting together in their platforms the interests of numerous groups across the country and thus trying to satisfy as many people as possible. Furthermore, it has been assumed that the party system, through the principles of cabinet responsibility, provides stable government over fairly long, predictable periods of time.

While there are elements of truth in these claims, students also should understand that because of the electoral system, it is quite possible for the party in power to have won decisively in some provinces but have had little success in others, thus indicating that it had not appealed to a wide spectrum of Canadian interests and was in reality not a national party. There is also evidence to suggest that political parties have deliberately aimed at winning heavily in certain provinces to the neglect of others, that they have tried to use ethnic differences to win an election, and that these campaign strategies have intensified regionalism and ethnocentricity.

The picture of political parties as unifying forces in Canada is further complicated by the appearance of third parties. Whatever the merits of these parties, students should understand that, as most recent evidence reveals, they have weakened the stability of federal governments and increased the frequency of general elections. Whether this trend is injurious to the political community, whether is has encouraged cynicism or apathy toward politics and government among Canadians, are debatable questions that should be considered.

It has sometimes been assumed that Canadians balance the party in power in Ottawa by voting for a different party in provincial elections, that this introduces party politics into federal–provincial relations and makes cooperation between the two levels of government more difficult. Students should understand that the provincial wings of most parties are autonomous and may disagree with the national organization, that the provincial parties will reflect regional interests, and that federal–provincial confrontations are caused primarily by the clash of these interests rather than by rival party politics. Students should understand, as well, that the politicians attending federal–provincial conferences must speak for the particular interests of their own electorate regardless of who is in power in Ottawa, and that they may press their own provincial views to the detriment of broader considerations. To this extent political parties and the electoral process may be regarded as divisive influences in Canadian federalism. How much responsibility for this situation can be attached to politicians and political parties and how much to the quality of their various electorates is a question that should be discussed.

Students should understand that many Canadians believe that political parties and federal governments are too much concerned with questions of national unity and survival. They argue that because of regional cleavages, the concentration of the French-Canadian minority in Quebec, and the pervasive influence of the United States, national political parties have devoted too much time and money trying to accommodate different regional, cultural, linguistic, and ethnic differences. In this process party politics may have intensified the very tensions they were trying to lessen; as a result, political parties have failed to develop long-term policies that would cut across regional and social cleavages and thus indirectly have a unifying influence. In an industrialized and urbanized country like Canada such policies would be economic ones and might lead to the development of political parties based on class.

Students should understand some of the evidence that supports this viewpoint of Canada. They should also ask whether election contests between class-based political parties, such as some other countries have witnessed, are likely to lessen or intensify tensions in Canada. What happens to the politically weak in a contest between organized numerical strength and organized financial power? Is there a danger in a democratic society that groups having sheer numerical strength could abuse their power and, if so, what might be the results? Are economic cleavages more or less easy to resolve than those based on territory, ethnicity, and culture?

5. Public opinion in Canada

What are "public opinions" and what are the most important factors that influence the public from time to time on specific issues?

To what extent do the basic features of Canada create divisions in public opinion, how significant are these divisions, and what effects do they have on the political community?

What evidence exists to suggest whether people in Canada are well or poorly informed on major public issues? Are other qualities more important in public opinion than specific, issue-oriented knowledge and viewpoints and, if so, what are these qualities and to what extent do Canadians possess them?

Are current trends making it more or less difficult for the public to be well informed?

How do Canadians view their power as individuals to influence political decisions and what appear to be the effects of this self-perception? What channels are available to the public for influencing the decision-makers in Canada, are these channels more available to some Canadians than others and, on balance, how important is public opinion in the decision-making process?

a) Students should understand that the word "opinion" refers to viewpoints on issues that are open to discussion, are debatable, and offer alternatives. An opinion becomes "public opinion" when it is held strongly by a group of people large enough to reasonably expect that it may influence what a government will do. Thus the term, at this time of writing, can be correctly applied to Canadian views about gun control, capital punishment, or a northern pipeline; it would be inappropriate to use the term to describe opinions about contemporary art or views held privately by a few individuals, neither of which are likely to affect government policy.

Thus students should understand that there can never be just one public opinion on any given issue; there must be differences of viewpoint and, therefore, the plural term "public opinions" is more useful.

Students should understand that, beneath the surface of conflicting public opinions, a healthy political community requires a minimum consensus among its members about a few basic principles. Students might discuss the question of the extent to which there is a basic consensus in Canada. In doing so, they should understand that a consensus gives a country whatever unity it has and that a political community cannot survive as a democracy without agreement of fundamental ideals.

b) Students should understand that in a democracy where the government is designed to be responsive to the people, public opinions are vitally important, not simply at election times, but throughout the intervening years. Political parties, interest groups, provincial and federal departments of government all employ a battery of public relations and advertising experts to analyse and try to mould public opinions. For obvious reasons, public opinions today can neither be formed nor expressed through direct dialogue, as was the case, for example, in the old New England town meetings. Thus, students should understand the critically important role of the mass media – newspapers, radio, and television – in the Canadian political community. They should also understand how important it is to maintain the democratic principle of freedom of expression and at the same time ensure that the mass media use their powers responsibly.

Through studies of the mass media, students should begin to understand the extent to which newspapers, radio, and television are fulfilling their responsibilities to society. Do the media, for example, provide sufficient information to the public or are they too much concerned with advertising revenue and thus with providing popular entertainment? Do the newscasters give adequate unbiased information on public issues, is the news slanted, is it too much concerned with entertainment trivia and sensationalism? Is it fair to indict the media on any of these counts? Do they simply provide what the public wants and, if so, should they cater to these desires? Does the responsibility really lie with the public and, if so, would better education and a more enlightened public improve the quality of the media?

c) Students should understand the great difficulties of either supplying or receiving information about public issues in a highly complex industrialized society. Many issues are so technical and the amount of information so voluminous that only the experts and a few deeply concerned individuals seem capable of understanding them. Semantics create another problem; there is no way of knowing whether the meaning attached to a word by a reader, viewer, or listener is the one intended. Students should understand the connection between all this and the tendency for elections to become personality contests, for the opinion-makers to neglect the issues and concentrate on emotional appeals and the building of images. Thus students should understand that without much access to expression through the media, with all the difficulties involved, and with vague feelings that they are being had, many Canadians may give up, become frustrated, alienated, or cynical and be content to leave politics to others. They should also understand that such attitudes can be injurious to the basic principles of democracy.

d) In spite of all these difficulties, students should understand that there are alternatives. Many issues are still within the comprehension of most Canadians; even without much information, a citizen sensitive to the fundamental principles of the Canadian political community can make wise decisions about even the most complex questions. Thus it might be argued that an understanding of the basic democratic ideals, and a willingness to live by them, is more important in determining the quality of public opinions than is detailed information about specific issues. Finally, students should understand that abundant information, frequently in less difficult form than commonly supposed, is available on even the most complex questions. In the mass media Canadians have the technical power to supply in-depth information to very large numbers of people, and if Canadians become sufficiently interested, better ways to use communications technology can be devised.

e) Students should understand that the basic features of Canada are important factors to be considered in any discussion of public opinions. They should understand that Canadians are exposed to the influence of the United States through radio, television, American-owned news gathering agencies, the movies, news magazines, and the operation in Canada of multinational corporations, most of which have public relations departments to advance their own particular views. Students should have some understanding of the amount of time Canadians devote to these American sources of information and the general effects this has on internal efforts to mould public opinions.

Students should understand that provincial and regional divisions in Canada have important effects on public opinions. They should understand that on many national issues there is a general tendency for public opinions to divide on provincial or regional lines. For example, there will tend to be underlying assumptions that influence public opinions in Alberta on all questions concerning oil, gas, and energy policies; or again, there will tend to be a general antipathy in both the Maritime and Western provinces toward any policies that seem to benefit central Canada disproportionately. They should also understand the particular position of Quebec, the tendency for public opinions there to concentrate on provincial matters, the growing desire to be *maîtres chez nous*, "masters in their own house," the difficulties of exchanging views with the rest of the country on questions of general concern, the isolation of the two main language groups from each other and thus the danger of serious misunderstandings. This danger is increased by the opinion of many English-speaking Canadians that Quebec is a monolithic society, and by Quebeckers' inclination to believe that the rest of the country speaks with but one voice, especially when it comes to questions concerning them. It is extremely important, therefore, for all students to understand that within any province or region there simply cannot be a single public opinion, that it is in the very nature of things for there to be two or more public opinions on any issue.

At this point, students might consider some additional questions about the media. Do the media act as divisive influences? Do they reflect unwarranted regional positions and thus intensify social cleavages, or do they usually express pan-Canadian viewpoints that contribute to greater understanding?

The multi-ethnic character of Canada's population also influences public opinions. Students should understand that when an issue seems to touch them closely, any ethnic group will tend to pull together and develop opinions based on ethnicity, especially if the group is concentrated geographically. Such ethnic opinions may be held with passionate conviction and may or may not be beneficial to the wider community. Keeping in mind the meaning of the term political community and the original Canadian ideal of establishing "a new political nationality" that transcended ethnic and religious considerations, students should understand the importance of and the need for significant, nation-wide issues that cut across linguistic, cultural, and ethnic lines. Thus, while recognizing the inevitability of such public opinions, class time should be devoted to identifying and weighing issues that are of common concern regardless of language, religion, ethnicity, and other factors.

f) As indicated previously, various opinion surveys indicate that the majority of Canadians believe they have very little political influence and that public opinions do not count for much. Students should understand it is easy enough for an individual to conclude that one vote among millions is of little consequence. With the issues so complex, the governments so large and remote, the search for individual recognition and security so difficult, feelings of alienation, frustration, and apathy are almost inevitable in any modern political community.

On the other hand, students should understand that votes do count, that public opinions remain very important in between elections, that governments do heed these opinions, and that there is access to the seats of political power. In connection with the last point, students should understand that through at least some of the roles they will have as citizens, opportunities exist for constructive participation in the political community. As members of a political party, a trade union, an environmental organization, or any one of the innumerable voluntary associations involving human relations that can put pressure on governments, they will have power to influence the political decision-making processes in Canada. With these opposing sets of understandings, students should be able to conclude whether or not the perception many Canadians have of their lack of political influence is valid.

6. Interest groups in Canada

What are interest groups and what are some of the most important ones in Canada? To what extent are these interest groups the products of the basic features of Canada? What are the differences between public opinions and interest groups?

In what ways do interest groups attempt to influence governments? What happens when different interest groups make conflicting demands on governments? How significant are interest groups in creating or relieving tensions in Canadian society?

a) Students should understand that interest groups are voluntary associations bringing together people with similar backgrounds, outlooks or "interests." With the democratic right to freedom of association, with man's natural desire to seek the fellowship of others, and with the range of interests almost limitless in our modern society, it is understandable that the number and diversity of these associations in Canada is tremendous and that they are an inevitable and desirable feature of our society. Interest groups vary from small local associations of tenants, for example, to national or international groups having large permanent staffs and substantial budgets, such as the Canadian Manufacturers' Association or the Canadian Labour Congress. Many groups continue in existence year after year while others are temporarily formed in response to some particular situation. A great many associations, probably the most important ones, are based on economic interests; others, having no specific economic base, may be cultural, religious, ethnic, and so on. Thus, students should understand that, almost inevitably, they will become members of one or more interest groups within the Canadian political community.

Students should understand that interest groups usually carry on a great many non-political activities of benefit to their members and to society. In addition, all of the more important groups attempt to influence the government; even those having no political purpose will suddenly become actively involved if they feel that their interests are threatened or can be enhanced by government intervention. This is such an important function that interest groups are sometimes called pressure groups, a term that probably overemphasizes their political activities. Students should understand that interest groups, as well as seeking to achieve their objectives through exerting pressure of various kinds on government, can also provide a number of valuable services for government. An interest group can be a source of useful, specific, and sometimes expert information; it can give good and unbiased advice; it can help the government, through its own organization, to implement and administer laws. There are, for example, many such close contacts between government departments and groups like the Canadian Bar Association, the Canadian Federation of Agriculture, the Canadian Tax Foundation, and others.

b) Students should understand that some interest groups will make demands of the government which will conflict with those of other groups and that it is up to the government to evaluate and make decisions about these competing demands. Thus the interests of conservationists may clash with those of the Newfoundland seal hunters; the interests of developers may be opposed by a local historical society; the interest of prairie farmers on tariff questions may not be shared by manufacturers in Ontario; some demands of the Canadian Labour Congress may conflict with those of the Canadian Manufacturers' Association; and so on. Students should understand, therefore, that some groups have more power to influence government than others and that the reasons for these inequalities are important considerations. In a democratic society governed by men seeking re-election, is sheer numbers the main source of power? How important is wealth, prestige, access to the media? Does dedication and determination sometimes make up for lack of numbers? When it comes to their own selfish interests, do those groups that have continuous contacts with government departments usually get their way? Can the power of reason or justice prevail over other considerations? Through the use of a few of the many examples available, students should be able to understand the reasons for the strength of some pressure groups and to identify the ones that appear to have the most influence in Canada.

It is important for students to understand that, however active and influential an interest group may be, there are many counterbalancing checks on its power. The very fact that the more important issues usually stimulate the activity of many interest groups, that the opinions of the general public must be considered, and that politicians can and do exert independent leadership, places restraints on any one group and tends to prevent extremism. Nevertheless, students should understand the possibility of an interest group resorting to extreme measures to achieve its goals.

c) Through readily available simple illustrations, students should understand that the following are among the legal ways used by interest groups to influence government: they can mount a publicity campaign and try to get public opinion on their side; they can persuade people to write to their members of Parliament; they can appear before parliamentary committees or various special commissions of investigation; they can submit annual briefs to the whole cabinet or try to establish close relationships with the individual cabinet minister responsible for their particular area of interest; they can try to persuade a political party to their way of thinking; they can try, by various means, to influence election results; and they can work through the bureaucracy. Considering how important the public service now is in the decision-making process, it is understandable that the most influential interest groups tend to be the ones having close, informal, continuous contacts with senior bureaucrats.

Students should understand that, although the contacts of many interest groups with the public service are maintained without publicity and behind closed doors, there is usually nothing sinister, illegal, or undemocratic about their activities. Senior public servants are supposed to know what they are doing, they are influenced by other pressure groups, they are also aware of public opinion, they have to sell their recommendations to cabinet, and cabinet ministers do have to consider their own party, the opposition, and the need to be re-elected.

On the other hand, students should understand that close relationships between interest groups and government do present opportunities for corrupt and illegal practices. Unfortunately, there are numerous cases at all levels of government of a pressure group buying influence through gifts of money, goods or services to

69

politicians and public servants. When one of these cases is exposed, usually by the media or opposition parties, sometimes by the police, there is a great outcry and much publicity that can cause unwarranted cynicism about politics. Students should understand that, considering the multitude of continuing legal relationships between governments and all the diverse interest groups, cases of bribery and corruption are comparatively rare and should not be allowed to distort the picture.

Students should understand that another difficulty, possibly more important than the detection, punishment, or elimination of corrupt practices, arises from the operation of powerful pressure groups in a society where thousands of people are not organized. How are these unorganized interests to be protected? During periods of inflation, what happens to consumer interests or retired people on fixed income in a society where both industry and labor are well organized to protect themselves? Is this imbalance, especially in the economic field, a major cause of social inequalities and possible injustice? If not, what safeguards are provided by the political system?

d) Students should understand that the basic features of Canada, the resulting federal structure of society, and the parliamentary system of government all affect the ways in which pressure groups are organized and operate. Most of the permanently organized pressure groups in Canada are themselves federations with provincial branches composed of many local groups. Depending in part on their particular interests and the division of legislative authority in Canada, some interest groups will concentrate their efforts at the provincial level and have strong regional bodies, some will be highly centralized to deal mainly with the federal government, while others find it advisable to work at both levels.

Students should understand that the parliamentary system of government in Canada is important in determining how interest groups try to exert pressure. Considering the way government policies are initiated and decisions made, it is understandable that attempts to influence individual members of Parliament or parliamentary committees usually are not as effective as working through the senior public service. Thus, in contrast to the United States where, at least in theory, lobbying by pressure groups is open to public scrutiny, the political activities of interest groups in this country are much less visible. Whether or not this opens the door wider for corrupt practices or unfair influence is a debatable question.

It is important for students to understand that because Canada is naturally exposed to many kinds of influences from the United States, there is an "American presence" in some of our most influential interest groups. The Canadian Manufacturers' Association in its deliberations must consider the views of multinational corporations with head offices in the United States. Likewise, many of the strongest unions affiliated with the Canadian Labour Congress are international ones having their headquarters across the border. Thus students should understand that, through the political activities of these and other interest groups, American viewpoints can influence the policies of the Canadian government. Whether or not these influences are always in the best interests of Canadian society is another debatable question.

70

Students should understand that many interest groups are formed along ethnic lines. Such groups are particularly active in areas that directly affect their own people, such as immigration, human rights, and education. Students should understand also that many interest groups professing to be nation-wide in scope in reality represent English-speaking Canadians only. They should understand that Quebeckers have created a large number of interest groups having little or no connection with so-called national organizations and that many of these groups deal exclusively with the provincial government in Quebec City. Whether this is a healthy situation, whether it gives English-speaking groups too much influence in Ottawa, whether Quebeckers lack influence at the federal level, and whether they are any more preoccupied with purely provincial affairs than other groups, are questions students should consider.

Students should understand that both the industrialization of Canada, and its particular resource base, are predominant factors in the development of interest groups. There are unions to speak for miners, lumbermen, steelworkers, electricians, plumbers, carpenters, and so on; there are groups to represent the primary producers, the mining industry, the forest products industry, the steel, chemical, publishing, and other manufacturing industries, all kinds of retail trade associations, and so on. In addition to these obvious interest groups, students should understand the connection between industrialization, the concentrations of population, and the proliferation of groups interested in urban problems. Also, they should understand that concern about the pace of resource use and rapid development has brought into existence a number of groups interested in conservation and the quality of the environment, and that these interests frequently clash with those of many other organizations loosely described as the developers.

Thus, through these and many other factors that might be considered, students should develop an overall understanding that the existence, nature, and activities of interest groups in the Canadian political community are primarily due to the interactions of the basic features of the country and that interest groups are inevitable sources of tension in society as well as constructive elements in the whole process of political life.

7. The structure and functioning of the Canadian government

What are the main components (legislative, executive, judicial, administrative) in the structure of the government of Canada?

What features make it a parliamentary democracy and how, in theory, is it designed to place ultimate power in the hands of the elected representatives of the people?

In practice, do current trends tend to place abnormal power in the cabinet and its various supporting executive agencies (such as the public service, the Privy Council Office, the Prime Minister's Office, executive assistants)?

In what ways do the basic features of Canada and the federal structure of the Canadian society impose practical constraints on the power of the Prime Minister and cabinet?

In the entire decision-making process how important is the influence of each of

71

the following: the cabinet, its various committees and executive agencies, public opinion, interest groups, the mass media, backbenchers on the government side of the House of Commons, opposition members of the House, senators?

To what extent do the basic features of Canada and the federal structure of society prompt ad hoc decisions based on day-to-day political accommodation between divergent, conflicting interests?

Considering the decision-making processes in the government of Canada, does the self-perception Canadians have of their power to influence the government seem to be a valid one?

a) Students should understand that the Canadian form of government is a parliamentary democracy and is based on the rule of law. They should understand that there are three basic kinds of governmental power: legislative, executive, and judicial; that in Canada legislative power is vested in a Parliament, composed of the House of Commons and the Senate; that executive power is vested in the cabinet, assisted by permanent officials known as the public service or the bureaucracy; and that the judicial power lies with judges and a system of courts known as the judiciary.

b) From studies of the role of the party in power in the House of Commons, of the ways in which the Prime Minister and other cabinet ministers get their positions, and of the principle of cabinet responsibility, students should understand some of the close links that exist in Canada between the legislative and executive parts of the government.

They should understand that the same basic principles of cabinet responsibility also exist at the provincial level. In other words, they should understand that, unlike the American system, the Canadian form of government is not based on a separation of legislative and executive powers. They should understand also that in the final analysis supreme legislative power does lie with the Parliament of Canada (or, within areas of their own competence, the provincial legislatures).

c) Students should understand that in the early history of democracies, there existed a deep suspicion of governments and a belief that, in order to ensure individual liberty, governmental activities should be kept to a minimum. They should understand that all of this has changed radically; governmental activities have increased dramatically and now affect the lives of all Canadians in a multitude of ways. They should understand some of the reasons for these developments and the corresponding phenomenal increase in the size, costs, and complexity of government. This understanding is so important that it should be illustrated as fully as possible with statistical evidence and specific examples.

d) Students should understand that the increase in governmental activities has greatly expanded the power and changed the character of the cabinet and public service; the executive branch (at both the federal and provincial levels) now legislates without recourse to Parliament, strongly influences legislative policies, and even interferes with the courts through the decisions of a multitude of boards and commissions. Students should understand why these developments in the government of Canada might be regarded as a threat to democratic procedures.

e) Students should understand that, although the power of the executive has been expanded greatly, there are a large number of counterbalancing forces at work within the political community. They should understand that the general climate of opinion and public opinions on specific issues in Canada do permeate and influence the public service and especially the cabinet; that the mass media, both in the expression and the formation of public opinion, is influential; that certain reforms of Parliament and party caucus are attempting to restore some lost powers to backbenchers; that the opposition parties, in the parliamentary question period, can take the government to task in front of the television cameras; that there is value in the deliberations of a non-elected body like the Senate; and that supreme legislative authority continues to rest with the elected representatives of the people.

Students should understand that among the factors curbing the power of the executive are internal differences within the cabinet and the party in power and that both reflect the federal structure of Canadian society. They should understand that, powerful though the Prime Minister's role is, he too is restricted by a number of constraints, most of which also reflect the federal structures of society and government.

f) In the light of this group of understandings, students should further consider the self-perception the majority of Canadians have as being without significant political power. They should understand that they will have many different roles as citizens of Canada and that some of these can provide opportunities either as individuals or in groups to influence governments. This thought, combined with an understanding of the pervasive effects of governments on the lives of all Canadians, should prompt a discussion of whether the feelings of alienation, lack of power, and political apathy that the majority of Canadians are said to have are self-defeating.

8. Intergovernmental relations

What is meant by the term federal–provincial relations? In what ways do the basic features and federal structures of Canada make continuing relations between the central and provincial governments an important part of the Canadian political system?

Why are there federal–provincial conferences at the ministerial level; at the first ministers' level? What factors have prompted a recent increase in the use of both types of conference as procedures for handling federal–provincial relations? What are some of the more important kinds of issues on the agendas of these conferences?

What evidence exists to suggest that these two types of federal–provincial conferences have witnessed a number of confrontations between the central and provincial govrnments? What issues seem to have provoked the most controversy at these conferences? What particular features of the federal structure of Canada seem to have intensified federal–provincial confrontations?

73

In addition to conferences of ministers and first ministers, what are some of the other procedures used in federal–provincial relations? How successful have these procedures been in securing cooperation between the levels of government? On balance, what danger is there in emphasizing the more visible confrontations that sometimes occur at major federal–provincial conferences? Are present trends both within the political system and in the Canadian environment leading toward greater or less stability in Canadian federalism?

What qualities or characteristics are needed by each of the following to ensure that the inevitable stresses of federal–provincial relations do not become too severe: public opinion in different parts and among different groups in the country; major interest groups; political parties; the mass media; technical experts in executive agencies; political leaders?

a) Building on their previous studies of the diversities in Canadian society and the reasons for a federal system of government, students should now try to understand the ideal that lay behind the union of the British North American colonies in 1867 – namely, that Canadians were forming a political community to achieve a limited number of common purposes that would require some allegiance and duties from all its citizens while at the same time providing ample scope for many individual and group diversities and loyalties.

Also from previous studies, students should understand that in order to achieve this, Canadians established a federal system with a written constitution defining the respective powers of the central and provincial governments. It was felt that the activities of the two levels of government easily could be kept separate, that they would operate only within the areas assigned to them by the constitution, and that any disputes could be resolved by the courts.

At first this system worked according to theory if only because difficulties in transportation and communication did in fact tend to isolate the central and provincial governments. Students should understand (in general terms to be expanded later through historical analysis) that, with the impact of the industrial revolution and the complete transformation of the Canadian economy from rural and isolated to industrial, national, and interrelated, a clear-cut division of powers between the federal and provincial governments became increasingly difficult. Thus today because of growing interdependence across the country and also because of the phenomenal increase in governmental activities demanded by the people, neither the federal government nor the provinces can act in any important area without affecting the welfare and interests of each other.

b) Using some specific examples, students should understand that each province and each regional grouping of provinces such as the Maritimes or the Prairies have their own special interests and that these do not always coincide with those of the federal government or other provinces. Thus students should begin to see that, extremely complex though they are, intergovernmental relations are vitally important and that the ways in which they are handled will determine the success or failure of the Canadian political community.

c) Students should understand that there is now a vast array of organizations for dealing with interprovincial and federal–provincial relations. Many of these are composed of public service personnel; meeting to consider detailed technical issues, they are more often than not successful. Other more highly publicized organizations involve federal and provincial cabinet ministers, much the most important one being the Federal–Provincial Conference of Prime Ministers and Premiers. Students should understand that these kinds of conferences, however well arranged they may be, provide no formula for reaching authoritative decisions. Such conferences proceed through very tough political bargaining (much like diplomacy in the field of international relations), and the chances of reaching agreement are seriously reduced by divergent interests and policies.

d) Students should understand that the major items on the agenda of meetings like the Federal–Provincial Conference of Prime Ministers and Premiers (and the most likely sources of dispute) deal with fiscal questions and constitutional reform. Although these are exceedingly difficult topics, students should understand, in general terms, that the federal government uses its taxing and spending powers trying to maintain nation-wide economic stability and full employment. They should also understand that the federal view of the right taxing and spending policies at any given time may conflict with the policies and priorities of one or more provinces. Conversely, provincial fiscal policies can work against federal efforts to manage the national economy.

Students should understand the extent to which provincial activities and hence costs have expanded enormously in areas such as education, intraprovincial transportation, health and welfare, and resource development; this expansion has led to increasing provincial pressures for more "tax room" and a greater share of federal revenues. They should understand that all of this is further complicated by the existence of richer and poorer provinces within the Canadian political community, that the federal government has a responsibility to try to overcome regional disparities, that the revenue for these efforts comes from the advantaged provinces, and that misunderstandings and rivalries seem, therefore, to be inevitable. Another important complication is the unique position of Quebec and the particular set of demands it places on the federal government, although students should clearly understand that Quebec has not been alone in demanding more power and money from the federal government.

In summary, students should understand the issues that presently cause federal–provincial conflict. They should understand that, without a formula for resolving the differences, without a clear-cut constitutional division of legislative powers, these disputes have been settled by hard political bargaining on specific issues. They might then consider whether this situation prevents the development of long-term national policies or, given all the circumstances, it is the only possible approach in a country like Canada.

e) Students should understand that, with all the difficulties in federal–provincial relations, a movement for reform of the constitution has developed. In raising the question of how the constitution of a federal political community can be amended a number of proposals have been discussed; however, it has proved impossible for the provinces and the federal government to agree on any formula to date. Students might then consider whether this failure indicates that Canadians do not really know what kind of country they want, and also whether the debates on constitutional reform have undermined confidence in the usefulness of the British North America Act without replacing it by anything else.

f) Students should understand that in the conduct of the federal–provincial relations at the political level, the elected officials feel compelled to act in accord with the desires of their own people and that these desires are expressed through the mass media, public opinion, the activities of interest groups, political parties, and in other ways. They should then consider whether changes in the attitudes and behavior of any or all of these groups would permit political leaders to conduct federal–provincial negotiations in more productive ways and if so, what changes seem appropriate and how might they be brought about.

(*Note:* This last point is expressed, not as an understanding, but as an open-ended discussion topic because there is ample room for reasoned differences of opinion. Undoubtedly some of the discussion should deal with the question of whether the schools have had a positive, neutral, or negative influence and whether changes might be made to strengthen the role of the schools.)

A study of the preceding sets of questions on these eight topics should give students some understanding of how the Canadian political system works. However, to enable students to examine the system in greater depth, the following sets of questions are presented. The questions posed under the headings Historical Analysis and Future Analysis are not accompanied by understandings. It is hoped they will serve as a guide to teachers wishing to pursue the study of Canada's political system further in the classroom.

B.   HISTORICAL ANALYSIS

9. *What reasons prompted the political leaders of the British North American colonies to create the Dominion of Canada in 1867?*

Which of the original purposes of the Fathers of Confederation are still operative, which ones appear to have dissipated, and what other goals, if any, have replaced them?

What evidence suggests that Confederation was an elitist movement without widespread public support? What difficulties have persisted in Canada as a result of these circumstances?

10. *What considerations prompted the Fathers of Confederation to adopt a parliamentary system as compared to other systems they might have selected?*

What features of the British North America Act most clearly reveal attempts to accommodate the basic features of Canada?

What features of the British North America Act indicate that the original intention of the Fathers of Confederation was to make the central government more powerful than the provincial ones?

For what reasons is the British North America Act still a very important document for Canadians?

11. *In general terms, what changes have been made in the powers of the Governor General and in Canada's constitutional relations with the United Kingdom since 1867, and why were these changes made?*

What constitutional powers concerning Canada remain with the government of the United Kingdom, why have those powers been retained, how important are they, and what can Canadians do about them if they wish?

12. *At what times and over what issues were there serious dominion–provincial confrontations in the period 1867–1918?*

What kinds of political activity did these confrontations produce?

What pattern or common set of causes appears in all of these "crisis" situations and what does this pattern reveal about the basic, federal nature of Canadian society?

What techniques were used to settle these crises, how satisfactory were the decisions, and what effects did the decisions have on the stability of Canadian federalism?

What are the similarities and differences between the federal–provincial relations in recent years and those of the 1867–1918 period?

13. *What considerations caused Canadians in the period 1867–1918 to look primarily to the federal government for leadership rather than to the provinces?*

What technological and other changes since 1918 have tended to reverse this situation, making the provincial government more important than formerly, and directing public attention more to the provincial capitals?

In what ways did the Great Depression and the Second World War still further alter federal–provincial relations?

What strategies and power has the federal government used since 1945 to invade areas that were formerly exclusive areas of provincial jurisdiction? Conversely, what strategies have the provinces adopted to challenge policies within federal jurisdiction?

Are federal–provincial confrontations more or less frequent and severe than formerly and is there more or less interprovincial and federal–provincial cooperation than formerly?

What are the arguments for and against a greater degree of decentralization of political power in Canada?

14. *Have political values and attitudes within Canada remained fairly constant over the years or have they changed and, if so, what caused the changes?*

Has the political behavior of Canadians remained fairly constant over the years or has it changed and, if so, what prompted the changes?

In what ways have the processes by which Canadians develop their political values and attitudes changed in recent years as compared to the period 1867–

1918? Do these changes mean that Canadians are more or less well informed about public issues than formerly or that the quality of public opinion has improved?

15. *What has been the significance of each of the following in the history of Canadian society: technological developments of the last seventy-five years; Canada's relations with the United States; anglophone–francophone relations; differences in viewpoint between the have and have-not provinces; immigration; the growth of big business and big labor unions; urbanization; the growth of big governments and the increased costs of all levels of government?*

C. FUTURE ANALYSIS

16. *Considering present trends, what changes in the basic federal nature of Canadian society might be predicted, what factors might prompt these changes, and what might be the overall effects on the political culture of Canada?*

Would such changes make it more or less difficult for the successful operation of the Canadian system of government?

What adjustments in the structure and functioning of the Canadian federal system of government may be desirable to accommodate the changing nature of Canadian society?

17. *What immutable factors will continue to exert a strong influence on the Canadian political community?*

What changes, if any, might be anticipated in the influence and significance of each of the factors listed in question 15 above?

18. *Considering the inevitable tensions present in all federations, will the Canadian federal system tend to be under more, less, or about the same degree of stress in the future?*

What conditions or circumstances might make it difficult for the Canadian political community to cope with future tensions successfully?

19. *Considering the present pervasive influence of governments on the lives of all Canadians, what future trends might be predictable; in other words, will the impact of governments on individuals and groups be greater, less, or about the same?*

CHAPTER VI

Studying the Canadian Economic System

The main purpose of this chapter is to develop understandings about the structure and functioning of the Canadian economy; it will examine the ways in which the economy has developed in response to the basic features of Canada, the kinds of demands it makes on the political system, the almost inevitable presence of conflict and tension in all economic demands, and the resulting need for continuous, complex political activity and decision-making.

The questions and understandings are not intended to provide a course in economics; rather they are designed to be a framework for studying one very important aspect of Canadian society in broad, general terms. It should be re-emphasized that the understandings are optimum learning outcomes, involving widely varying degrees of sophistication, and should not be regarded as a rigid program for all students. Economic ideas, relationships, and terminology are more complex and probably less familiar than those associated with the political system. Although all understandings should be covered to some extent, the program described in this chapter may require one to make more adjustments to the abilities of individual students than does the study of Canada's political system.

Despite its vital importance to any real understanding of Canada, the study of the Canadian economic system has never held a prominent place in our schools. Nevertheless, the importance of this subject to all students who, in one way or other, are going to be part of the labor force in a modern community, requires a reassessment of the ways in which it may be studied in our schools. A formal or traditional course in economics is not necessary to provide students with some initial understandings of Canada's economic system and its relationship to the political processes and decisions that directly affect the lives of all Canadians.

UNDERSTANDING THE CANADIAN ECONOMIC SYSTEM

A. CONTEMPORARY ANALYSIS

1. Human needs and economic systems

What are the main characteristics of human wants and of economic resources that motivate all economic activities?

What is the fundamental economic problem facing all mankind?

To what extent does the problem vary in Third World countries as compared to the more developed nations?

a) Students should understand that the fundamental economic problem facing any country or the world community as a whole is somewhat similar to that of an individual family. The members of the household bring home pay cheques of fixed amount, but the family has many needs, sometimes more than the pay cheques will cover. Thus decisions must be made about how to spend a limited resource (money) on a multitude of family needs. In society, money is only one of many resources: there are non-human resources such as farm land, trucks and trains, factories, mines, pipelines, and power plants; and there are human resources such as skilled labor or highly trained scientists. Students should understand that these resources – the factors of production as they are called – are scarce, and that they can be put to many different uses. Farm land, for example, can be employed to produce food or it can be subdivided for suburban housing.

Students should understand also that, although some families may be able to satisfy all of their wants (there may be such a person as the man who has everything), the wants of a society as a whole are unlimited. The *desires* of society, as distinct from what its members really *need* for physical survival, apparently are not only insatiable but also capable of tremendous expansion through technological change and the power of advertising. For example, no one wanted television sets fifty years ago for the simple reason that there were none.

Using these two ideas, students should understand that the central economic problem for all societies is to allocate scarce resources in such a way as to satisfy as many wants as possible; obviously this involves making choices and sacrifices. For many years, the Soviet Union, for example, devoted so much of its resources to the production of industrial and military equipment that it was unable to satisfy many of the ordinary consumer needs of its citizens. Likewise, it is possible for a country to build so many office skyscrapers that insufficient resources are available for housing. Students should understand that the basic choices made by any country will determine what commodities will be produced, by whom, and with what technologies, and who will reap the benefits from their production.

Students should understand that all nations have some kind of an economic system. In industrialized countries, this is composed of a complex set of practices and institutions involving such things as commercial and central banks; transportation and communications networks; many different kinds of business and labor organizations; stock, bond, and money markets; mechanisms to determine prices, wages, rent, and interest rates; and so on. All of these are designed to resolve the basic economic problem of satisfying as many human wants as possible with scarce resources.

b) It is very important for students to understand that Canada is one of the two or three richest nations in the world. Although Canada's resources, like those of all other countries, are limited and Canadians must make choices from their many desires, the choices they have to make are entirely different from the ones facing two-thirds of the world's population. Many people in the developing countries of Central and South America, Africa, the Middle East, India, and parts of Asia live in abject poverty, ill-health, and ignorance, facing the constant threat of malnutrition, with populations always pressing on the resources for bare existence; their choices (to the extent that they have any) are in terms of physical survival. Canadians, living in a country free to take advantage of all the benefits of industrialization and technology, a country richly endowed by nature with many different resources and with capital to invest in economic growth and human welfare, enjoy one of the highest living standards in the world. Although pockets of real poverty continue in Canada, the economic choices facing most Canadians are luxurious and beyond the dreams of the majority of the world's people.

Students should understand the significance of some of the available evidence that shows the difference between the rich and poor nations, between the affluent and consumption-oriented societies like their own and the poverty-stricken and survival-oriented societies of so much of the rest of the world. They should consider what obligations the rich nations have toward the developing countries and to what extent Canada and other developed countries are attempting to meet these obligations.

2. National income in Canada

What does the term national income mean? How is competition within the market system intended to distribute this income?

What are the advantages and disadvantages of the market system for distributing Canada's national income?

What factors influence economic growth and, therefore, national income?

What are the costs and benefits of economic growth as a national goal for Canada? Why has there been growing government intervention in Canada's market economy?

a) Students should understand that people who want to use any factor of production must pay for it. Those who need the services of a doctor, lawyer, or plumber must pay fees or wages; doctors or lawyers who need office space must pay rent to the owners of office buildings; those who want to construct office buildings must pay for land, construction materials, transport facilities, skilled workers, architects, and consultants. Bread companies, meat packers, and whiskey manufacturers may pay the farmers to produce some of their raw materials and the farmers, in turn, must pay for their machinery. The sum total earnings of these and all the other factors producing goods and services in Canada can be regarded in simplified terms as the national income.

81

Students should begin to understand that, in a country like Canada where most of the factors of production are owned privately and where government control of the economy is limited, competition is one of the most important determinants of how the national income is distributed. The share of the national income received by individuals or groups of Canadians (such as wage-earners) is decided by the "market system" or, preferably, by many different markets where the supply of and the demand for resources, goods and services all interact to determine prices. Through the use of simple examples, students should understand as fully as possible that Canadians either individually or in groups compete with each other as buyers and sellers, as part of *both* the supply and demand side of the market system.

Students should understand that this built-in competition to get as large a share of the national income as possible inevitably causes tensions in society and that, from one point of view, the Canadian economic system is motivated by self-interest. Assuming for the moment that the economy is not expanding, it is obvious that an increased share gained by one group must be at the expense of some other group.

Students should understand that inflation can be caused by unwarranted increases in the costs of production ("cost-push" inflation) or by excessive demand driving up prices ("demand-pull" inflation) or some combination of these two. In other words, inflation can be caused by companies and labor unions seeking higher profits or wages and also by insatiable consumer demand. It is important for students to understand the effects of inflation not only on obvious groups such as the poor and pensioners with fixed incomes but also on whole sections of the Canadian economy. For example, inflation is causing Canada's export industries to lose their competitive advantage in world markets and this, in turn, can adversely affect all Canadians in the long run.

Students should recall what they have learned about interest groups and how such groups attempt to advance their own interest – usually trying to get a larger share of the national income – by exerting various pressures on governments. Thus, they should understand more fully the dangers in a competitive society with limited resources and insatiable demands when powerful economic groups press their own interests without due consideration of the consequences for society as a whole.

In addition to the distribution of the national income among the major factors of production – the share received in the form of wages, salaries, returns to farms and unincorporated businesses, interest, rent, and corporate profits – students should also understand distribution in terms of family incomes in Canada. Although the available evidence supports the view that Canadians generally have one of the world's highest standards of living, the problems of unemployment and poverty are serious ones in Canada. Either the market system does not provide enough jobs for those who want to work, or their services command such a small wage that they cannot live decently. Students should understand some of the ways in which minimum living standards and poverty are defined and realize that, regardless of definition, far too many Canadian families live in poverty.

Finally, students should understand that, if they need detailed information about how the national income is distributed, it is readily available through Statistics Canada, the Economic Council, and other government agencies in the form of graphs, charts, and columns of figures. While this kind of information can be useful, students should clearly understand that all statistics must be analysed very carefully because they can be interpreted in many ways and used to support almost any economic argument. In this connection, it is important for students to understand that in a regionally divided country like Canada, national statistics need to be supplemented with regional breakdowns because such things as hourly wage rates and standards of living vary greatly across the country.

b) Students should understand the commonly held assumption that the only way Canadians can improve their standard of living and reduce the problems of unemployment and poverty is by increasing the size of the national income – that is, by stimulating growth in the economy. Real economic growth can be achieved by increased investment in the factors of production, the more efficient use of existing resources, or some combination of the two.

Students should have an in-depth understanding that the productivity of the Canadian people (human resources) is dependent on such things as education, social values and attitudes, motivation, mobility, age, health, and so on. The productivity of non-human resources (capital) can be increased through improved organization and management skills, certain economies resulting from increased size ("economies of scale") and perhaps, above all, by the introduction of new technologies through research, innovation, and risk-taking. At this point it is important for students to understand that the productivity (efficiency or quality) of Canada's human and capital resources lags well behind the productivity of some other industrialized countries. This has serious consequences for the economy, including such things as a high cost of living, difficulties of competing in world markets, and the probability of further inflation whenever an economic group gets a larger return without an increase in efficiency.

Students should understand some of the advantages and disadvantages of economic growth. A growing economy can provide higher standards of living, reduce the incidence of unemployment and poverty, and above all create the tax base from which governments can increase the amount of what is called "social capital" – that is, money which is spent on such things as schools, hospitals, roads, museums, libraries, parks, and recreational facilities. Students should also understand that such things as the pressure of population growth on the world's resources, the rapid rate of resource exploitation by the industrialized countries, the non-renewable nature of many vital resources, and urban congestion have prompted many people to question the wisdom of economic growth or at least to recommend improvements in the quality of growth.

c) Students should understand that the preceding picture of the Canadian economy needs to be counterbalanced by other considerations. The Canadian economic system, looked at from another viewpoint, is composed of a vast complex of interlocking mechanisms that require a great deal of cooperation for their smooth operation. Students will understand something about this intricate system if they consider even some of the many cooperative economic

83

activities required to fill the daily needs of any large Canadian city – activities that most Canadians take for granted. Against this background, they should understand that the Canadian economy simply could not work without co-operation between all its different parts.

3. The free enterprise system in Canada

What are the legal foundations of the free enterprise system?

In theory, how does this system work to resolve the competing interests of the various economic groups in Canada?

In practice, what developments have tended to prevent the free market forces from functioning as they are supposed to do?

As a result of these developments, is the economic system more or less just to society as a whole than it was formerly?

a) Students should understand that despite the growing importance of government in practically all phases of human experience, free enterprise is still the basic characteristic of the Canadian economic system. The principle legal foundation of the free enterprise system is private property: that is, the right of individuals to control their own property, including their labor. In theory, Canadians are free not only to own the instruments or factors of production but to use them as they wish for personal economic gain. This means that all economic activity is carried on in an atmosphere of competition and that the motivating force throughout the whole economy is the desire for economic rewards or profits.

In very general terms, students should understand that economic competition is between the sellers and buyers of resources, goods and services; that the amount of a resource or product offered by sellers (the supply) and the amount buyers are willing to pay (the demand) determines price; that the price at which goods can be produced and sold determines profit; that profits regulate the production of resources, goods and services; and that the "market" where supply and demand (sellers and buyers) meet to determine price does not really exist. The market is many markets, operating without central control or planning, usually without any physical location, and functioning through the millions of small decisions to buy or sell, to produce or not to produce, that all Canadians – businessmen, workers, and housewives – make hour by hour, day after day. Students should understand that, according to theory, this market system in which people are competing for their own economic rewards is supposed to function for the benefit of all Canadians.

Students should understand that the market system works only when the owners of the means of production can make a profit. In the final analysis, it is the consuming public that determines profit and, therefore, how the resources of Canada are used.

b) Students should understand that the free enterprise or market system does not always operate according to theory. This is due, not to any overt conspiracy of capitalists against the general welfare, but to structural and other weaknesses in the system itself. The market system assumes conditions of open, fair, or "pure competition." In practice, such conditions hardly ever exist because many individuals and groups have little or no real bargaining power while others seem to have too much.

Students should understand the reasons for the competitive disadvantages in the labor market of groups such as fishermen, farm workers, unskilled and poorly organized industrial workers, the tens of thousands engaged in service industries (janitors, waiters, store clerks, garage attendants), recent immigrants, and all those who are unable or unwilling to move to where there are better job opportunities because of linguistic and cultural considerations. All of these and other groups have little influence on wages; they must take what they can get.

Students should understand that the market system, because of the advantages of mass production and other economies of scale, encourages the growth of big companies. Naturally, small firms competing in the same industry with large corporations usually are at a disadvantage. It is important for students to understand the viewpoint that since many of the largest corporations in Canada are multinational, with head offices usually in the United States, many smaller Canadian-owned firms may have difficulty competing in the market place. Furthermore, it is possible for one giant corporation (or more likely a very few corporations) to dominate an industry. Under these conditions of monopoly or quasi-monopoly, prices are determined within broad limits by a few powerful corporations and not by competition in the market place.

Students should understand that the theory of consumer sovereignty is also undermined by the power of suppliers through advertising to manipulate lifestyles and consumer tastes and demands. Thus it is possible to argue that in many instances what is produced and how Canada's resources are used is determined by the owners of the means of production whose decisions may or may not be beneficial to the long-term welfare of society. At the same time students should understand that in a free enterprise system the consuming public can resist the power of advertising, they can refuse to buy, and they usually do have choices.

It is particularly important for students to understand that there are many essential goods and services the market system will not provide simply because their production would yield no profits. This includes things such as hospitals, roads, and schools, to which reference has been made previously under the heading of social capital. Social capital and associated services must be supplied by governments from taxes. Students should understand that in a free enterprise system, the private sector must flourish in order to provide the tax base for these kinds of governmental activities.

Students should understand that the market system, left to its own devices, does not always operate smoothly and that there are recurring cycles of prosperity and recession. More importantly, they should understand the impact of these cycles, especially in terms of idle and wasted human and material resources.

Finally, students should understand that the market system sets up interprovincial rivalries and that some provinces enjoy competitive advantages over others. Some provinces, because of their favorable location, lower transportation costs, suitable resource base, and adequate skilled labor are able to attract an increasing number of businesses and continue to grow economically. Further-

85

more, these favored provinces have a stronger tax base from which they can provide more social capital and services. Thus the market system in part has created richer and poorer provinces within Canada so that regional economic disparities are a continuing national problem.

c) Students should understand that the three levels of government intervene in the Canadian economy in a sustained effort to counterbalance the defects in the free enterprise system. This helps to account for the phenomenal increase in government activity noted previously in studies of the Canadian political system. While this is much too complex a subject for any kind of detailed investigation, students should have some understanding that the poor, the unemployed, the aged, and other groups lacking bargaining power are protected by such things as unemployment insurance, minimum wage laws, family allowances, and old age pensions. Farmers are assisted by price-support programs, marketing boards, surplus purchases, funds for rural rehabilitation, and agricultural research programs. Small businesses and the general public are at least partially protected against monopolies and quasi-monopolies by fair practices legislation and laws against combines in restraint of trade. Consumers are protected by pure food and drug acts, research and publicity (such as the hazards of smoking), laws to protect the environment and prevent false advertising, and by a multitude of other regulations. Regional economic disparities are partially balanced by various kinds of federal grants and special programs for depressed regions.

Students should understand that all of these government activities must be financed by taxation and that governments now take a substantial part of the gross national product in various kinds of taxes. Students should have some understanding of current figures showing the billions of dollars spent by governments and the percentage of the gross national product devoted to government activities.

d) Students should by now understand that the Canadian economy is a mixture of public and private enterprise and that with so much government enterprise and control it is appropriate to describe Canada's economy as a mixed rather than a free enterprise system. Students should recall what they have learnt about the division of opinion between those who favor more government intervention and those who believe in preserving as much free enterprise as possible. This issue should now be studied from an economic perspective rather than a political one as previously. Students should be provided with as much hard, unbiased evidence as possible so that they may begin to understand the range of alternatives available, the reasoning used to support both democratic socialist and free enterprise policies, and the costs and benefits involved.

4. Sectors of the Canadian economy

What are the major sectors of the Canadian economy and what degree of emphasis, in terms of labor and capital, is placed on each one?

What sectors of the economy appear to be under-emphasized, what are the main causes of this imbalance, and what effects does it have on Canadians?

What measures might be initiated to correct present imbalances between the various sectors of the Canadian economy?

a) Students should understand that the Canadian economy is regarded as having two very broad divisions. These are the public sector – which includes the economic activities of the government – and the private sector – which includes all the rest of the economy that operates under the principles of the free enterprise system. Leaving the public sector for later consideration, students should understand that the private sector has three basic divisions: primary industries, secondary manufacturing industries, and tertiary industries. A preliminary understanding of these three sectors may be gained from the following simple examples. A company that works on the extracting and refining of bauxite ore to make aluminum is in the primary sector of the economy; a company that uses the aluminum to manufacture outboard boats is in the secondary manufacturing sector; and the tourist resort owner who rents aluminum boats to fishermen is in the tertiary sector. Similarly, a company mining or refining gold is in a primary industry; a company using the gold to make jewelry is in a secondary manufacturing industry; and a store that sells the jewelry is in a tertiary industry.

Students should understand that the primary sector consists of all industries directly involved in the extraction and processing of Canada's natural resources. It includes activities such as the various kinds of mining, lumbering, farming, fishing, and related processing industries such as smelting, oil refining, pulp and paper, flour milling, canneries, and so on. (Primary industries are frequently described as resource-based industries.) As the name implies, secondary manufacturing industries are a stage removed from those in the primary sector. They include the making of such things as automobiles, electrical appliances, machinery, tools, household goods, and all the other products that require the raw materials of the resource-based industries. Tertiary or service industries include transportation and communications, advertising, wholesale and retail merchandising, service stations and garages, hotels, restaurants, all kinds of financial institutions, and a great many other industries or occupations that provide services to people.

b) Students should have some understanding of the tremendous importance to Canada of the resource-based industries. Of these, the mineral industry has been for many years the most significant factor in Canada's economic growth and still is the main force in the northward advance of her frontiers. The mineral industry includes metallic minerals such as nickel, lead, zinc, copper, iron, and gold; non-metallics such as asbestos, potash, sulphur and salt; fuels such as coal, gas, and crude petroleum; and structural materials such as clay, sand, and gravel. All in all, Canada has most of the minerals needed for modern economies; it leads the world in mineral exports and is third largest producer of minerals.

Students should understand that some of the most difficult questions facing Canadians arise in this sector of the economy. Some natural resources such as forests, farmland, fish, and wildlife, if exploited under proper control and management, are renewable. All of Canada's mineral wealth is non-renewable; once used it can never be replaced. The mineral industry is a costly and risky business requiring capital investment in exploration for new sources of raw materials, expensive machinery, high failure rates, and the inevitable exhaustion of mines, oil, and gas fields. For these reasons, governments until recently have encouraged the mineral industry with subsidies, exemptions from income taxes, and various other incentives.

Students should understand that these incentives, beneficial though they are to the mineral industry, have encouraged many mine owners to work their mines as hard as possible – to hasten the exploitation of non-renewable resources – during the so-called tax-holiday period. It has also been argued that government taxation and incentive programs have led to an over-emphasis on natural resources at the expense of manufacturing which creates many more jobs. It is true that Canada would be better off in terms of income and employment if it had developed the manufacturing industry that could use all of its raw materials. Because the domestic market is small and Canadian manufacturing with a few exceptions cannot compete with other more efficient industrialized countries, Canada does not use most of the minerals presently produced. Its surpluses are exported primarily to the United States and more recently to Japan, thus helping to pay for imports from abroad. Even so, some Canadians believe that the country's natural resources, especially the non-renewable ones, should be left in the ground until our domestic industries need them.

Students should understand that this highly controversial question is complicated still further by the fact that a large part of the mineral industry in Canada is foreign-owned. This has led to the additional argument that Canada is being stripped of its non-renewable resources to feed the factories of countries like the United States and Japan where some mineral shortages are becoming acute. When discussing this question, students also should consider that the mineral industry, which has contributed so much to the economic growth of Canada, probably would not have been developed to its present levels without money from other countries and that exports of primary products are essential to pay for all the things Canadians cannot make or grow for themselves. In addition, they should understand that governments have recently cut back many incentive programs and that these measures have had a depressing effect on the mineral industry.

Students should understand that the control of natural resources and resource-based industries is a major cause of interprovincial and federal–provincial disputes. Under the terms of the British North America Act, all natural resources belong to the provinces in which they are located. This helps to explain still further the existence of regional economic disparities and the strong differences of opinion between the have and have-not provinces over tax-sharing and other federal–provincial agreements. Equally important is the fact that the federal government, through its control of foreign trade and its taxing powers, can interfere with provincial rights in natural resources. This raises the serious question of the extent to which the federal government, acting in the interests of all Canadians, should interfere with any province that happens to be rich in essential natural resources.

Students should understand that the exploitation of natural resources raises a whole range of environmental and conservation questions. As a starting point, they should understand that until recently most people assumed Canada's supply of natural resources was virtually unlimited and that the quality of the environment, especially pure air and water, could be taken for granted. With increasing industrialization and the ever-accelerating pace of resource use, these assumptions are both invalid and dangerous. Renewable resources must be carefully controlled by industry and governments. Although there is a long way to go, questions of this kind associated with renewable resources are now receiving much more attention than formerly.

Although projections of resource use and existing reserves are conflicting, students should clearly understand that some Canadian resources, particularly oil and gas, may be in short supply or exhausted within their own life times. Since supplies of energy are so vital to all modern economies, students should investigate this question as thoroughly as time will permit. In doing so, they should consider the pros and cons of reducing economic growth rates, changing life-styles and consumption patterns, or accepting the popular view that man has the technological skill to develop alternatives for any non-renewable resource.

From a different perspective, students should understand some of the environmental problems arising in the primary sector of the economy. Although they are by no means alone, pulp and paper companies have been accused of seriously polluting northern rivers and lakes; insecticides used to protect farm crops and forests have done great damage to some forms of wildlife and food supplies; emissions from smelters have polluted the air and killed vegetation in surrounding areas; lumbering companies have been careless in their reforestation and clean-up operations, and so on. In any discussion of these kinds of problems, students should again consider that large resource-based companies have tremendous engineering skills; also that there is a continuing need to find new sources of raw materials. Only by considering as much evidence as possible from all sides in these controversial issues will students begin to understand how difficult it is to develop satisfactory resource-use policies.

c) From previous work, students should have begun to understand that the secondary manufacturing sector of the Canadian economy is not as strong as it might be. This is unfortunate; manufacturing industries provide more jobs and higher average wages and also lead to the growth of population centres and thus stimulate service industries in which the majority of Canadians earn their living. There is no doubt that Canada has the natural resources for a much stronger manufacturing sector and more of these resources could be processed domestically rather than being exported in their raw state. Students should understand the significance of the fact that although Canada is foremost in the world in the export of many metals, it is a net importer of products manufactured abroad from our nickel, aluminum, copper, and other raw materials.

Students should understand that the usual reasons given for weakness in the secondary manufacturing sector is the small size of Canada's domestic market. This is only a partial and unsatisfactory explanation. Mass production and economies of scale – the ability to spread the fixed costs of production over a great many units – do not depend entirely on having a huge market. A smaller company with lower fixed costs (for buildings, equipment, and so on) can also benefit from economies of scale even though it is producing for a smaller market. Furthermore, it can be argued that the market for manufactured goods is world-wide and that efficient companies are in no way restricted to the domestic market.

Students should understand that a great many of Canada's secondary manufacturing industries are not competitive in world markets. Not only can other countries undersell Canadian products abroad, they can do so right in Canada. This is particularly evident in electronic components, computers, pharmaceuticals, scientific instruments, man-made fibres, and other industries that require a high degree of scientific knowledge, technology, and innovative ability. Canada's poor performance in the rapidly expanding, profitable science-intensive industries means that we are not particularly inventive or innovative, that we are not as technologically advanced as is commonly assumed, and that we are content to import most of our scientific know-how.

Students should understand that some of the difficulties in the secondary manufacturing sector are associated with the operations of multinational corporations in Canada. It is understandable that many branch plants of foreign-owned corporations will rely on research and development done by their parent companies and that they will import sophisticated components rather than encouraging production in Canada. This means that such branch plants have a competitive advantage over Canadian-owned companies who must try to do their own research and development (or import it) and also that opportunities in some of the world's most rapidly growing industries are seriously limited. Furthermore, many industries in the secondary manufacturing sector are dominated by two or three large, usually foreign-owned corporations that have the lion's share of the market. A number of smaller companies (frequently too many) compete for what is left over. Thus the Canadian market is still further fragmented and weakened.

Students should understand that industrial wage rates and worker productivity have some influence on the ability of Canadian industries to compete in world markets. For many years, wages in Canada lagged well behind those in the United States. Now a large percentage of Canadian industrial workers receive wages that are equal to or exceed those in the United States. Combined with this development is the fact that in many industries – chemicals for example – Canada invests more money in capital equipment per job than any other country in the world. This combination of capital and labor has not resulted in greater productivity. While managers of capital may blame workers and vice versa, the fact remains that most manufacturing companies in Canada operate with higher costs and less efficiency than those in the United States.

Students should understand the significance of the relationships between Canada's primary and secondary manufacturing sectors. This is extremely important for Canada's long-term economic prospects and raises a number of critical value questions. If present trends continue, the evidence suggests that of all Canada's non-renewable resources only coal and iron will last more than one hundred years, while crude oil and other vital ones will be in short supply long before that time. Thus, it is quite possible that many of Canada's resource-based industries may not be able to compete in world markets in the future. With declining revenues from exports, Canadians will have great difficulty paying for all the things they buy from other countries. Considering the weaknesses in the secondary manufacturing sector, it is unlikely that Canadians could pay for their imports by selling manufactured goods in world markets. These considerations suggest that Canadians should take whatever steps are necessary to develop an internationally competitive manufacturing industry.

d) Students should understand that tertiary industries are particularly important in terms of employment. Including the major divisions of transport and communications, wholesale and retail trade, financial institutions, insurance and real estate, and the strictly service industries such as hotels and restaurants, more Canadians work in the tertiary sector than in all the primary and secondary manufacturing and construction industries combined. Furthermore, the percentage of the labor force working in the primary and secondary sectors is either remaining constant or declining. While there are other reasons for this situation, the most important one is associated with technological developments. The number of Canadians working in agriculture, for example, has fallen dramatically over the years, yet agricultural production has increased. In other words, fewer farmers using modern machinery and scientific methods can produce much more than formerly. Improvements in technology also help to account for the drop in the percentage of Canadians working in manufacturing and the levelling off of employment in other primary industries.

Students should understand that some tertiary industries are expanding rapidly. With the percentage increasing every year, one of every three Canadians in the labor force now works in service industries such as gasoline stations and garages, repair shops of many kinds, marinas, tourist resorts and other recreational facilities, hotels, restaurants, dry-cleaning establishments, laundries, and other similar occupations. Because these kinds of jobs require little skill or education, people working in many tertiary industries are among the lowest-paid groups in Canada.

Thus, in summary, students should understand that as Canada becomes more industrialized and work more automated and as the population continues to grow, an increasing number of Canadians will have to find employment in the tertiary sector. Within this sector at present, the industries that are growing fast enough to absorb a larger percentage of the labor force are those requiring mainly unskilled workers.

5. Foreign economic relations and the Canadian economy

For what reasons and to what extent is foreign trade vitally important in the Canadian economy?

In what ways is Canada's foreign trade particularly vulnerable relative to that of many other countries?

What evidence can be used to show the predominant position of the United States as Canada's major trading partner and what are the main reasons for this predominance? What are the advantages and disadvantages for Canadians of the present foreign trade position with the United States?

a) Earlier in this chapter students have had a number of opportunities to develop some understanding of Canada's position as a trading nation. This section, therefore, is partly a review – a putting together of understandings acquired indirectly through other studies of Canada's economy.

91

Students should understand that international trade is vitally important to all countries and especially one like Canada whose standards of living would be drastically reduced without imports and exports. Although Canada does some business with virtually all countries, it is the United States that buys most of Canada's exports and supplies the great bulk of all her imports.

Students should recall that Canada's export trade is primarily, but not exclusively, in agricultural and forest products (especially pulp and paper) and all forms of raw or semi-processed minerals. Since all mineral products are non-renewable, questions of conservation and resource use have become critical. These questions are complicated by the fact that American companies control many of Canada's mineral resources and that the United States is by far and away the major consumer of such products. Therefore, one of the most controversial issues facing Canadians concerns the wisdom of continuing to export resources that can never be replaced. Throughout any discussion of this issue, students should be aware that exports are essential to pay for all the things Canada imports and that the living standards of Canadians would be adversely affected by a decline in export trade.

Students should recall what they have learned about Canada's secondary manufacturing industries and why most of them are not competitive in world markets. This means that Canada is in the incongruous position of heavily importing from the United States many products made directly from her own natural resources. Thus, for example, we are the world's second largest producer of aluminum but we import it in forms such as sophisticated aluminum parts for aeroplanes; we export large quantities of gas and petroleum but these are more than balanced by imports of petrochemicals; we are the world's largest exporter of pulp and paper but we import many kinds of paper products.

Students should recall that the preceding considerations have raised the question of Canada fully processing more of her resources and trying to develop an internationally competitive manufacturing industry. Students should understand, however, that all industrialized countries want to export as many manufactured products as possible and that the world market for manufactured goods is extremely competitive and requires sophisticated technology and scientific knowledge for success. It is precisely in these science-based industries that Canada, with a few notable exceptions such as heavy generating equipment, is unable to compete. In many high technology industries – the industries of the future as they are sometimes called – the United States is the world leader. Whether Canada should attempt to compete in these industries or be content to continue importing much of its technology is a debatable question.

Finally, students should understand that for more than one hundred years Canada has had a tariff policy to protect her industries from foreign competitors. The Canadian tariff is in reality a vast set of varying taxes, many the result of trade agreements with other countries, that Canadians must pay on most goods purchased abroad. The purpose of these taxes, of course, is to encourage Canadians to buy Canadian-made goods and thus protect domestic industries and jobs. While the tariff undoubtedly does this, it is also obvious that Canadians, in order to get things they cannot buy in Canada or that are cheaper and possibly better made elsewhere, import what they want and pay the taxes. All of this adds to the cost of living in Canada because customs duties naturally are passed on to the consumers in the form of higher prices.

Students should understand that in the nineteenth century the tariff was defended on the grounds that it protected Canada's small, "infant" industries from large American competitors who had a long head-start. Now that Canadian industries have had decades to grow and mature, this argument has been replaced by one that claims Canadian companies need to be protected from poorly paid foreign labor. Some businessmen and workers, for example, complain that, in order to protect the higher standard of living in Canada, these cheap, foreign goods should be excluded by high tariffs. This is a dubious argument because Canada has a favorable trade balance with Japan (in other words, we sell more to them than vice versa) yet wage levels there are much lower than in Canada. Students should also understand that, as long as Canada maintains her tariff, other countries will tend to retaliate against her exports.

b) Students should understand that, in addition to the export and import of goods, Canada has a great many other economic relations with foreign countries. Canadians travel abroad, spending money as they do so, and foreign visitors come to Canada; foreigners invest in Canadian companies and expect to receive interest or dividends for the use of their money; Canadian provincial and municipal governments borrow money in the United States because it is usually cheaper than borrowing in Canada, and must pay interest on their loans. These and many other items determine Canada's balance of trade with foreign countries.

Students should understand that Canada has always had a favorable balance of trade in goods, or in "visible" trade as it is sometimes called. This means that Canada exports more than she imports. This favorable balance, however, is more than offset by "invisible" items such as the payment of interest and dividends to foreigners who have invested in Canadian companies and in Canadian provincial and municipal bonds. When all the items are taken into account, Canada usually has an unfavorable balance of trade. In part, this is a reflection of the tremendous amount of foreign, mainly American, investment in Canada and the resulting need to make large interest and dividend payments abroad.

In general terms, students should understand some of the consequences of Canada's balance of trade position. When Canadians go to Florida in the winter, they must take American money with them; when Americans invest in Canada they receive interest or dividends in their money; and when American exporters sell goods to Canadians they expect to be paid in American dollars. Conversely, Canadians are paid for the goods and services they sell to foreigners in Canadian money. In a very complex way, all these transactions create a supply of and a demand for Canadian and American dollars. This money market works in much the same way as any other market. When Canada has an unfavorable balance of trade with the United States there will be a heavy demand for scarce American dollars to pay for all the goods and services Canadians are buying from that country. This will tend to drive up the price of American dollars so that Canadians, instead of paying $1 Canadian to $1 American, may have to pay more of their own money to buy an American dollar. When Canada has a favorable balance of trade with the United States, Americans will have to pay out slightly

93

more of their money to buy a Canadian dollar. These fluctuations in the rate of exchange between Canadian and American dollars are exceedingly important in the total volume of business between the two countries.

Students should understand that when the exchange rate is favorable to Canada – when the Canadian dollar is worth more than the American – Americans will tend to buy less from Canada. This has adverse effects on the tourist trade and on Canada's vitally important exports. The resource-based industries are especially hard hit. On the other hand all those, including governments, who have borrowed in the United States will benefit because it does not take as many Canadian dollars to pay interest or dividends to American creditors. When the exchange rate moves against Canada – when the Canadian dollar is worth less than the American – the preceding results are reversed. Americans will be encouraged to travel in Canada and to buy more from Canada, while it will be more costly for Canadians who have to make interest payments to Americans. The important point is that exchange fluctuations affect various industries and parts of Canada in different ways and can cause serious dislocations.

6. Multinational corporations and the Canadian economy

What are multinational corporations, why have they come into existence, and what are the main types of such corporations?

What are some of the major multinational corporations operating in Canada, who owns them, and where are their head offices? In what sectors of the Canadian economy do foreign-owned multinationals appear to be particularly prevalent?

What are the advantages and disadvantages for Canadians of the operations of foreign-owned multinational corporations? In particular, is the expansion of a multinational corporation usually financed by imported capital or by retained earnings in Canada?

In what ways do the attitudes of Canadians toward foreign-owned corporations vary in different parts of the country and what are the reasons for these differences in attitude?

a) Students should understand that a multinational corporation is a form of business organization designed to operate on a world-wide scale. These firms, many of which have head offices in the United States, have complete or majority control over any companies they establish or purchase in other countries, so that the business activities of all their branch plants or subsidiaries are part of a vast international production and marketing plan. There are many foreign-owned, mainly American, multinational corporations doing business in Canada.

Students should understand two ways in which foreigners can invest in Canada. American investors, for example, might buy Ontario Hydro *bonds*. This means that they have lent money to Ontario Hydro; they expect to get their loan back sometime and to be paid interest. However, these loans do not give Americans voting rights or any other form of control over Ontario Hydro. Another kind of foreign investment is the purchase of *shares* in a company. As the name implies, this gives the investor a share in the actual ownership of the company and voting rights as to how it will be managed. This is the form of investment used by multinational corporations so that they have controlling interest in all of their Canadian subsidiaries. Unlike bonds which can be redeemed, direct foreign investment in stocks gives continuing ownership and control over some part of another country's assets.

Students should understand that for many decades Canada has relied on money from other countries to build railways and power dams, develop her natural resources, and so on. Without foreign investment in earlier years, it is unlikely that the Canadian economy would be as far advanced as it is now or that Canadians would enjoy their present high standard of living. Foreign investment in Canada grew comparatively slowly, however, until after the Second World War when multinational corporations made their appearance as a new form of business organization and spread rapidly throughout the world. These corporations, especially the American-based ones, found Canada an attractive country in which to invest. Canada was close at hand, secure and free from disturbing revolutions, friendly and very rich in natural resources. As a result, direct foreign investment in Canada in recent years has been increasing at the phenomenal pace of well over one billion dollars annually, so that today Canada has the highest degree of foreign ownership of any industrialized country in the world.

Using some of the statistics readily available, students should understand the extent of foreign ownership in key industries of the Canadian economy such as oil and gas, mining, forest products, rubber and automobiles, chemicals, electric equipment, and food processing. They should be aware of some of the more obvious multinational giants operating in Canada, such as the Ford Motor Company, General Motors, Chrysler, Goodyear Tire, Firestone, and others in the automotive and related industries; Crown Zellerbach, B.C. Forest Products, Reed Paper, Canadian International Paper, and others in forest products; Imperial Oil, Shell, Gulf Oil, Texaco, and others in oil and gas; Canadian Industries, Dupont, Union Carbide, and others in the chemical industry; Swift, Kraft Foods, Standard Brands, and others in the food-processing industry.

Students should understand that Canada has its own domestically based multinational corporations such as International Nickel, Alcan Aluminum, Labatt's and, perhaps best known of them all, the Canadian Pacific. Some industries such as steel, brewing, and liquor-distilling are dominated by large Canadian-owned corporations: Algoma Steel, Dofasco, and Stelco in steel; Seagrams and Hiram Walker–Gooderham and Worts in liquor; and Molson's and Labatt's in brewing. Furthermore, some sensitive parts of the Canadian economy such as banking are protected from foreign ownership by government regulations. However, with notable exceptions of this kind, students should clearly understand that a great many important industries in Canada are dominated by multinational corporations with head offices in other countries.

Students should understand that a multinational corporation can buy out or control another company without owning all or even a majority of its shares. This is because almost all companies have a great many small, widely scattered shareholders who have virtually no chance of coming together to attend shareholder meetings or to influence company policy. Thus the company can be effectively controlled by one or a few large shareholders. This makes it all the easier, of course, for multinational corporations to extend their interests and to set up such complex relationships between the parent company and its different subsidiaries that the layman has great difficulty knowing who owns what. Canadians own about 30 per cent of the shares of Imperial Oil, for example, but the remaining 70 per cent is owned by Exxon Corporation in the United States. Over 50 per cent of the shares of Hudson's Bay Oil and Gas (a good Canadian-sounding name) is owned by the Continental Oil Corporation in the United States. This list could be greatly expanded and made very much more complex. The important point is that ownership and control are well disguised within the structure of the multinational corporation.

b) Students should understand that government policies have encouraged foreign investment in Canada. The tariff, by making it more expensive to import manufactured goods from the United States, induced American firms to set up production facilities in Canada. Many federal and provincial policies to stimulate, by grants and subsidies, the development of slow-growth areas made no distinction between Canadian and foreign-owned companies. Canada exercises fewer controls over foreign firms than most other countries. Resource-based industries have received generous tax concessions, low royalty payments for the use of Canada's mineral and forest wealth, and a great deal of government assistance to build transport facilities to reach remote resources. In other words, it would be unrealistic to blame foreign-owned multinationals for their economic power in Canada because they have been warmly encouraged to invest in this country.

Students should understand that in the early years of industrialization, Canadians may have needed foreign investment for economic developments they could not afford themselves. In recent years, however, the operations of foreign-owned multinationals have been so successful that their continued expansion in Canada has been largely financed from profits made in this country. Furthermore, Canadians have invested some billions of dollars in other countries. Some experts are of the opinion that, except for huge projects like the James Bay Development Corporation, Canada now has sufficient money to finance her own economic growth and no longer needs foreign investments for a healthy economy.

Students should attempt to evaluate the advantages of foreign-owned multinational corporations. A great many Canadians believe that multinationals are good corporate citizens of this country. They create job opportunities with good wage rates, most of them employ Canadians in middle-level and top management positions, they invest part of their profits in the continuing expansion of the Canadian economy, they contribute to Canadian charities and a wide variety of community and university projects. Perhaps above all, they provide access to very costly, sophisticated technologies that Canadians might never have been able to afford themselves. Using as much evidence as possible, students should understand the on-going controversy between Canadian economic nationalists and continentalists about the degree of Canada's dependence on the economy of the United States.

c) Finally, students should understand some of the effects of multinationals, Canadian or foreign-owned, on the theory that prices are set by free competition

96

in the market place. Although the theory remains valid in some parts of the economy, it is out-dated in all Canadian industries that are dominated by two or three large corporations. Considering modern industrial methods, a corporation like General Motors or Westinghouse must spend large sums of money before it even begins production. It must have decided what it thinks the public wants and the price at which it will have to sell in order to cover costs fixed in advance and to make a profit. With so much money involved, a large corporation simply cannot take chances. Therefore, it advertises heavily to ensure that the public really does want what it has produced. None of this involves a conspiracy of large corporations against a gullible and easily manipulated public. It is simply a consequence of the structure of North American industry as presently constituted.

From the preceding considerations, students should understand that the use of Canada's natural resources is largely determined, not by long-term social policies nor the basic needs of the consuming public, but by the decision of large, usually multinational corporations. They should also understand that Canada is an affluent, consumption-oriented society and that, if some resources are squandered on frivolous consumer goods, the general public must assume part of the responsibility. Some Canadians are now suggesting that this country should abandon continued economic growth as a national goal, and that it should move away from a consuming society toward a "conserving" society. Students should understand some of the widely divergent views on this and other questions concerning the future of the Canadian economy.

7. Regional disparities and the Canadian economy

What are regional economic disparities, what evidence can be used to show the existence of severe economic disparities in Canada and what parts of the country are most adversely affected?

To what extent are regional economic disparities caused by natural factors and to what extent by man-made decisions?

What are the reasons for the great concentration of economic activity and wealth along the lower lakes between Windsor and Montreal?

What evidence indicates that the concentration in this area is intensifying and what are the likely effects of this trend on the life-styles of the inhabitants and on the Canadian society as a whole?

a) Through previous work on both the political and economic systems, students should have already developed an understanding that regionalism is a very important, if not the most important, of the basic features of Canada. Regional economic disparities, which have been a major continuing concern of Canadians since Confederation, merit more detailed study than has been devoted to them up to this point.

Students should understand that national statistics on such things as hourly wage rates, family income, unemployment, and so on become much more meaningful when broken down into provincial or regional figures. Unemployment for Canada as a whole, for example, may be 8 per cent of the labor force, but in some parts of the country it may be very much higher. Using current statistics for regional income per capita, family income, unemployment, percentages of the population below the poverty line, the quality of education, and social services and other data, students should understand the severity and incidence of regional economic disparities in Canada.

Students should understand that the poorer provinces simply do not have the tax base to provide the same social capital and services as do some of the other provinces. Thus the depressed regions do not have as much money for schools, roads, hospitals, recreational facilities, civil service salaries, public works and, as a result, the living standards of the people are lowered still further. Students should understand the importance of providing equal opportunities for all Canadians, regardless of where they live, to participate in the economic growth of the country and that this national goal has never been achieved. They should also understand that not all Canadians have the same values and that to some extent economic disadvantages may be offset by more attractive life-styles.

Students should understand that facts and figures tell only a small part of the story and that regional economic disparities have deep psychological effects on the people living in both depressed and affluent provinces. Thus, in the Atlantic provinces and in parts of Western Canada, while there is a great deal of regional pride, there is also some evidence of feelings of inferiority and a certain resentment of the central provinces. Conversely, in those provinces where things are going reasonably well, there is a tendency to ignore the existence of regional economic disparities and a failure to recognize that the problems of any one part of the country should be the concern of all Canadians. Students should consider the extent to which these and other regional feelings and attitudes arising from economic circumstances are injurious to the Canadian political community as a whole.

b) Students should understand why some provinces are so much richer than others. While attention should be directed to all parts of the country, this study should focus on the reasons why central Canada, especially the Great Lakes–St. Lawrence Lowlands area, has many economic advantages that the Atlantic provinces and parts of the Prairies do not possess. Although some of these advantages are the result of man-made decisions and might have been adjusted by different policies, most of them are due to natural, geographic reasons.

Students should understand the importance of geographic location, closeness to large markets, proximity to the industrial centres of eastern United States, access to cheaper water transportation, the quality of the soil and climate for agricultural purpose, the availability of natural resources such as mineral, fossil fuels, hydro-electric power, and forest reserves, the way certain resources complement each other as, for example, do timber reserves, hydro-electric power, and the pulp and paper industry.

Students should understand that industrialization promotes the growth of cities and that urbanization, in turn, brings larger domestic markets, a greater pool of labor, more and usually bigger companies, more social expenditures and amenities, expanding populations, all of which stimulate increased industrializ-

98

ation and create a snowball effect on economic growth. Thus, once started in central Canada, industrialization has produced its own dynamic, while the Atlantic region and some other parts of the country have tended to remain in the economic doldrums.

Students should understand the major man-made decisions that have intensified regional economic disparities. Some of these decisions were due to the greater influence in the federal government of the more populated central provinces; others were more or less predetermined by the basic features of the country. Students should clearly understand that the tariff policies first introduced shortly after Confederation have tended to benefit the central provinces at the expense of the Prairie and the Atlantic provinces. Also, students should understand that many transportation policies have intensified economic disparities. The original Intercolonial Railway, built to open central Canadian markets to Maritime products, had the opposite effect by exposing small eastern industries to competition from Ontario and Quebec. The Great Lakes canal system, especially the St. Lawrence Seaway, has stimulated economic growth in central Canada while bypassing the Maritimes. The major international airports have been built in Ontario and Quebec. During the war years most of the government contracts were awarded to larger companies located in the industrial heartland, thereby encouraging still further industrialization and urban growth in this region.

Finally, students should understand that technological developments can benefit some regions and be very detrimental to others. A classic illustration is the destruction of the so-called golden age in the history of the Maritimes by the increased use of iron ships and steam power. The natural relationships between the automotive industry and steel and nickel manufacturing or between hydroelectric power and the pulp and paper and aluminum industries, for example, have caused great economic concentration in Ontario and Quebec.

c) Students should understand that for all the preceding reasons, central Canada is continuing to grow economically at a much faster pace than other parts of the country. Although Edmonton, Calgary and Vancouver are expanding rapidly, Toronto, Montreal, and the Great Lakes–St. Lawrence Lowlands region are the industrial and financial centres of Canada.

In general terms, students should understand that industrial and urban concentration raises the question of life-styles and quality of life for the people in the big cities. Students should understand that urbanization brings a multitude of economic, social, and cultural advantages. Urbanization also brings gigantic problems of traffic control, waste disposal, air and water pollution, suburban sprawl, population diversities, human strains, land-use policies, increased crime, inner-city poverty, and so on. Students should consider some of the main costs and benefits of urban growth and question whether policies to decentralize industrial development are either desirable or feasible in Canada.

d) Students should understand that the federal government has tried in various ways over the years to lessen regional economic disparities. Since Confederation the federal government has spent huge sums of money building or subsidizing the construction of canals, railways, airports, and highways and developing communications networks such as the postal system and the Canadian Broadcasting

Corporation. While all of these have facilitated the movement of commodities, people, and ideas across the country, they have tended to benefit the prosperous regions as much if not more than the depressed ones. Lower freight rates on railways have been designed to help Prairie farmers ship grain to British Columbia or the Lakehead and to lower transportation costs to and from the Maritimes. The railways, of course, must be subsidized from the federal treasury for the lower rates. These measures have helped to balance disadvantages of distance but they have not lessened regional economic disparities.

Students should understand that federal welfare programs such as old age pensions, family allowances, and unemployment insurance, although national in scope, are especially beneficial to poorer areas. Unemployment insurance is more important to regions with high levels of unemployment just as old age pensions mean more to low-income families in the Maritimes than to the families of industrial workers in Ontario. Of greater significance are the tax-sharing agreements whereby the federal government, under a very complex formula, provides the have-not provinces with "equalization payments" to compensate them for their lack of tax revenues. These payments make up a large portion of the revenues of the poorer provinces. Even so, neither welfare nor equalization payments have appreciably reduced regional economic disparities. The per capita tax revenues of Manitoba, Saskatchewan, and the four Atlantic provinces are still far below the national average. Students should also understand that the provinces putting up the money for equalization payments (Ontario, Alberta, British Columbia) always resist any effort by the have-not provinces and the federal government to increase the tax-sharing formula.

In general terms, students should understand that the federal government has tried a great variety of ad hoc measures, usually on a cost-sharing basis with the provinces, to reduce regional economic disparities. These include such things as irrigation projects to assist prairie farmers, reclamation of marsh lands in the Maritimes, subsidies to depressed mining, fishing, and forestry industries, incentives for industries to locate in designated depressed areas, the encouragement of urban growth in the poorer provinces, the building of technical schools, manpower retraining programs, and many others. Despite all of these continuing and costly efforts, the gap between the richer and poorer provinces has tended to remain constant over a fairly long period of time. Federal programs have undoubtedly prevented the gap from becoming greater but students should clearly understand that severe regional economic disparities are an on-going problem within the Canadian political community.

8. Unions and the Canadian economy

What are labor unions, what types of labor unions exist in Canada, how is each union organized and financed, and how are the unions federated provincially and nationally?

What are the relationships between labor unions and federations in Canada and those in the United States?

What are the objectives of labor unions and what various methods do they use to achieve their objectives?

What methods are used by employers to counter union tactics? What means does society possess to promote industrial peace and how effective are these procedures?

a) Students should understand that the labor force in Canada is composed of all people 14 years of age and over who are able and willing to work. The labor force includes doctors, lawyers, factory managers, professional athletes, farmers, fishermen, teachers, industrial workers, store clerks, and an infinite variety of other occupations. Some members of the labor force have joined together in associations called trade unions (or labor unions) to promote their economic and social welfare through collective, rather than individual bargaining with employers. One out of every three Canadians in the non-agricultural labor force belongs to a trade union. All others operate in the labor market as individuals. Some of these, such as doctors, engineers, or lawyers do well in the labor market because of their education and specialized skills; others, such as non-union workers in the expanding service industries, have little individual power.

Students should understand that the main purpose of a labor union is to give its members bargaining power in negotiations with employers about wages, hours of work, overtime pay, job security, holidays, pension plans, and other working conditions. Compared to half a century ago, unionized workers in Canada today are living far better than their fathers or grandfathers ever would have dreamed. Students should have some understanding of the improvements in working and living standards in such areas as hours of work, real wages, holidays, pensions, factory conditions, and the material comforts that the average worker enjoys as part of the good life in Canada. Undoubtedly, these improvements in material welfare are partly due to the effectiveness of unions in bargaining with employers.

Students should understand, however, that the standard of living of unionized workers and other Canadians is the result of many factors and that it would be incorrect to attribute good wages and working conditions solely to union activity. The development of Canada's natural resources has contributed to the increase in the real wages of Canadian workers. Canada has had access to the money needed not only to produce all kinds of consumer goods but also to build factories, refineries, smelters, machinery, and other job-creating capital equipment. Furthermore, Canada has had the money to invest in social capital so that today's workers are better educated, more skilful, and healthier than their ancestors. The phenomenal growth in technology, whether imported or domestic, has led to rapid industrialization and urbanization and greatly enhanced the living standards of most Canadians.

b) Students should understand that there are two basic types of unions and that each one has certain advantages and disadvantages for both workers and employers. A craft union is an association of workers based on their particular skill or craft, such as plumbers, carpenters, electricians, and welders. Thus, a number of unions would be represented in a factory organized along craft lines. An industrial union is an association of all workers, no matter what they do, employed in a certain industry, such as the manufacture of automobiles. Thus, in an automobile factory organized along industrial lines all workers – janitors,

101

night watchmen, painters, assembly-line workers, and so on – would belong to one union. This means, of course, that an industrial union such as the United Automobile, Aerospace and Agricultural Implement Workers of America has the power to speak for all the workers, for example, in every plant of General Motors or Massey-Ferguson in Canada. Although craft unions lack this overall power, they can represent and speak for skilled workers in one indispensible part of the companies' operations. Frequently, there is intense rivalry between these two types of unions to organize workers in Canada.

Students should understand that most craft and industrial unions are composed of many branches (or locals as they are called), each with its own officers, distributed across the country. The sum total of members in all the locals make up a particular union, each of which has a national executive of elected officers. Unions in Canada may be national or international. As the names imply, national unions are composed of totally Canadian membership, while international unions have members in Canada and the United States, with head offices invariably south of the border. There are well over one hundred international unions in Canada; two-thirds of unionized Canadian workers belong to international unions.

Students should understand that, in addition to national and international craft or industrial unions, there are also federations of unions at the municipal, provincial, and federal levels. The great majority of national and international unions are affiliated with the Canadian Labour Congress (CLC); some unions, mainly French-speaking ones in Quebec, are affiliated with the Confederation of National Trade Unions (CNTU). Most of the international unions are affiliated with both the CLC in Canada and with the gigantic Congress of Industrial Organizations (CIO) in the United States. Although collective bargaining and other economic powers lie with individual unions, the political influence of municipal and provincial federations and especially of the CLC is substantial.

c) Students should understand that federal and provincial labor legislation contains provisions to prohibit any form of discrimination by unions or employers; to ensure equal pay for men and women doing the same work; to set standards concerning hours of work, overtime pay, minimum wages, safety conditions, holidays with pay, and a great many other items. With the consent of the provinces, the federal government has control over unemployment relief and retirement pension plans. (Quebec has its own pension plan.) The Unemployment Insurance Act is a compulsory plan to protect workers from loss of wages due to unemployment; employers and employees contribute to the plan. The Canada Pension Plan provides a retirement pension at age 65 and other benefits for virtually all members of the labor force; it is also financed by joint contributions from employers and employees.

Students should understand that federal and provincial labor legislation includes many provisions to regulate industrial relations – that is, to set out the bargaining rights of employers and employees. The most important of these provisions are the following: Every person is free to join a trade union; before it can negotiate with an employer, a trade union must be certified as the legal bargaining agent desired by the majority of workers in a plant; the union and

102

the employer are meant to bargain in good faith and try to reach a collective agreement that is embodied in a written contract. Before resorting to either a strike or a lock-out, both sides must agree to use some form of compulsory arbitration. Only after direct negotiations and arbitration under a conciliation officer fail, does a strike or lock-out become legal. During the course of a strike, unions and management must follow rules, the most significant one being not to use coercion or violence.

Students should understand that in negotiations between unions and employers, the ultimate weapon is the strike or lock-out. Over 90 per cent of all collective agreements in Canada are reached by direct negotiation or compulsory arbitration. When strikes do occur, especially in certain essential industries, they receive a lot of publicity, thus creating the false impression that labor relations are always in a turmoil. Even so, strikes are very costly to both workers and employers, they sometimes are illegal and violent, and they are used more frequently in Canada than in many other industrialized countries.

d) Students should have a preliminary understanding of some of the issues in contemporary industrial relations in Canada. One of the most important of these is the right to strike in industries that provide essential goods or services such as public transportation, hospital care, teaching, postal services, police and fire protection, and others. Workers in most of these industries have only recently received the right to strike – a right that is now being challenged in some circles.

Students should understand that another controversial issue is the extent to which trade unions help to cause inflation. Even in times of rising unemployment, many unions have been successful in bargaining for what appear to be substantial increases in wages for their members. Some unions have demanded and received wage parity with workers in the same industry in the United States. Considering that worker productivity in Canada is generally about 20 per cent lower than in the United States, successful demands for parity have inflationary effects. Furthermore, when economic activity slows down, unions seldom will consent to wage reductions. This helps to cause a rigid price structure and lay-offs by companies that cannot afford high wages in depressed times. For these and other reasons, the evidence suggests that unions are one of a number of economic institutions that can put upward pressure on costs and prices. Students should recall that many corporations, especially the multinationals dominant in some industries, also have the power to cause what is called cost-push inflation. Furthermore, the apparently insatiable demands of an affluent society, through demand-pull effects, must be regarded as an additional cause of inflation.

Students should understand that as businesses grew larger and more powerful so also did trade unions grow in size and strength. When two such powerful groups bargain with each other, the free competitive market system based on the supply of and the demand for labor may no longer exist. Both sides have somewhat monopolistic, balancing powers and can determine wages and prices with little concern for market conditions. This situation has prompted the belief held by some people that unions and businesses have become too big and that together they are injurious to the best interests of society as a whole.

e) Students should understand that at any given time, some members of the labor force will be unemployed; that is, they are willing and able to work but are unable to find jobs. Even under the best of conditions, there will always be some unemployment, if only because the labor force is mobile and people are temporarily out of work as they shift from one job to another. Owing to the climate, seasonal unemployment also is a serious problem in Canada. Certain kinds of work simply cannot be done during the winter months, so that the number of unemployed in January, February, and March is usually much larger than in the summertime. Unemployment in Canada, therefore, is always calculated on a "seasonally adjusted rate" to show what unemployment would be without the ups and downs due to the weather. Because there is always some unemployment, a seasonally adjusted rate of 3 per cent or less is regarded as full employment of the labor force. Unfortunately, the unemployment rate is frequently much higher than 3 per cent. Despite the protection of the Unemployment Insurance Act, the presence of so many jobless people in the labor force is a costly waste of human resources and a serious problem for Canadians.

9. The role of governments in the Canadian economy

What powers does the federal government have to control the economy and why is the use of these powers necessary?

For what reasons and in what ways does the federal government intervene to redistribute the national income?

In what other major ways and for what reasons do governments interfere with, regulate, or control the economic life of Canadians?

What are some of the ways in which governments try to assist various sectors of the Canadian economy?

What are some of the most important businesses that are owned and directly or indirectly operated by governments? Why is Canada regarded as a mixed economy and why has this kind of economic system developed in Canada?

a) In previous sections of this book, students have had numerous opportunities to develop understandings of the tremendous extent to which governments participate in the Canadian economy. Although this unit contains several important new concepts, it should be regarded partly as a review – a putting together of understandings acquired indirectly through other studies of the Canadian economy.

Students should recall that although the free enterprise or market system is still the basic feature of the Canadian economy, all three levels of government use their respective taxing, spending, and other law-making powers to intervene in and influence the economic system in a multitude of different ways. Thus the Canadian economy is broadly divided into the public sector and the private sector and is correctly called a mixed enterprise system.

Students should understand that almost any major piece of legislation is designed to achieve several objectives. The Unemployment Insurance Act, for example, was introduced to protect those who cannot find employment, and it should be regarded, therefore, as one of many measures to redistribute the

104

national income. At the same time, it also provides an element of stability and price support by putting some purchasing power in the hands of people who, in earlier times, would have been flat broke. Similarly, all welfare programs, in addition to their main objective of providing income for those who cannot fend for themselves, also act as a cushion to prevent prices from falling as tragically as they did in the Great Depression of the 1930s when such protective legislation was non-existent.

b) Students should understand that governments engage in a great many activities which are not, strictly speaking, economic, although they have important economic consequences. Governments provide police and fire protection, collect garbage, clean streets, maintain armed forces for national defence, establish embassies and consulates abroad, support all kinds of cultural activities, give different forms of aid to Third World countries, conduct investigations, engage in research, prepare and publish a multitude of reports, and so on. Considering the total range of all government activities, it is apparent that they require a huge staff of permanent, salaried employees known collectively as the public service. One in five Canadians now works for governments at either the municipal, provincial, or federal level. This means that in addition to all their other costs, governments have a very large payroll to meet.

Students should clearly understand that almost all of the activities of governments, economic or otherwise, have a price tag and that the public pays for them in the long run. As the range of government services and activities expanded rapidly after the Second World War, so the costs of government rose almost astronomically. At present, all levels of government combined spend more than $45 billion annually, an amount that represents about one-quarter of all annual spending in Canada. The money to finance these large expenditures is raised primarily by government borrowing and by a number of different kinds of taxes. Other sources of revenue include profits from government-owned businesses and compulsory contributions by employers and employees to government pension and unemployment plans.

Although the Canadian tax structure is very complicated, students should have some understanding of the major taxes levied by governments. These would include personal and corporate income taxes, sales taxes, succession duties, and property taxes on land and buildings. Considering the amount of revenue raised by it, the single most important tax in Canada is the personal income tax. This tax is graduated; that is, the tax rate or percentage of income taken by the government is small or non-existent for people on low incomes and becomes progressively higher for people with larger incomes. Many Canadians do not pay any income tax; others may pay anywhere up to 60 per cent of all they earn to the government in income taxes. It is apparent, therefore, that the income tax is an effective tool for the federal government to achieve the goal of redistributing the national income. It takes large sums of money from middle- and upper-income groups; some of this money is given to the lower-income groups in the form of family allowances, pension supplements, and other welfare payments. Personal income taxes are levied by both the federal and provincial governments.

Students should understand that all businesses in Canada, large or small, pay corporation taxes. These taxes also are levied by both the federal and provincial governments. The combined tax rate varies from year to year but is generally in the 45 to 50 per cent range, although small businesses and certain manufacturing companies do not pay as much as this. After taxes, a corporation may pay out some of its earnings in dividends to shareholders. Most of these dividends are taxable income for the shareholders and, in view of many Canadians, this is a form of double taxation.

Students should understand that next to personal taxes, the greatest source of revenue for governments is sales taxes. The federal government levies four different kinds of sales taxes: a general sales tax (presently 12 per cent) on a wide range of goods manufactured in Canada or imported from abroad; an excise tax on particular kinds of goods such as cigarettes and alcoholic beverages; a special or extra excise tax on certain "luxuries" such as jewelry, cosmetics, and wines; and custom duties or tariffs on goods imported into Canada. In addition, all provinces except Alberta have their own retail sales taxes. Although some necessities such as children's clothing, agricultural products, and heating fuels are exempt, the combined incidence of federal and provincial sales taxes on all Canadian taxpayers is very substantial. Provincial governments also collect succession duties or inheritance taxes and all property owners pay taxes to their municipal governments on the assessed value of land and buildings.

Students should understand that in addition to the taxes noted above, governments collect money from individuals and businesses in a great variety of other ways, such as licences for automobiles, medicare premiums, compulsory contributions for workmen's compensation, unemployment insurance and pension plans, place of business tax, mining and lumbering fees, and so on. And, of course, the general public pays to use some of the social capital of the country in the form of transportation fares, charges for municipal water supplies and hydro-electric power, fees for camping and other recreational facilities, and postal services. Taking all the different forms of taxation into consideration, Canadians are among the most heavily taxed people in the world. This is partly due to the sheer size of the country and to the federal nature of our society and government. It is also due to the high expectations of Canadians and the demands they have made on government.

Students should clearly understand that in a mixed enterprise system, the private sector must prosper in order to provide the investment capital and the tax base for the security and other social benefits Canadians presently enjoy. Students should consider the possibility that even with a prosperous economy, people might expect too much from governments and attempt to live beyond the country's means.

c) Students should understand that all three levels of government also raise money by borrowing either for short periods throughout each fiscal year or for a much longer term. Long-term loans are made by selling bonds to the public; the purchaser of a bond is in reality lending money to the government and is paid interest for the use of his funds. In peacetime, the main reason for long-term government borrowing is to pay for social capital. Since public works such as canals, power dams, highways, schools, and so on cost a great deal of money collectively and yet last a long time, it would be completely impractical to pay for them with taxes collected in any one year. For this reason, governments usually cover the costs of social capital by borrowing on a long-term basis. Governments also borrow when their annual expenditures exceed their revenues; this kind of borrowing also adds to the public debt. A substantial portion of the taxes collected each year by all levels of government must be used therefore to pay the interest on their long-term or bonded debts. Regardless of any other pressing needs, these annual fixed charges to service the public debt limit the freedom of action by governments to a certain extent.

Students should understand that government borrowing is a normal business practice and does not mean that governments may go bankrupt, provided the economy continues to grow. On the other hand, students should recall that provincial and municipal governments do much of their borrowing in the United States mainly because interest rates are usually lower there. Interest payments to American purchasers of municipal and provincial bonds are a drain on the country's assets and contribute to the difficulties in Canada's balance of international payments. In general, the public debts of governments in Canada are not as serious as is sometimes believed and in no way can be compared to an individual who is badly in debt. However, students should understand that continued excessive borrowing by any level of government – witness New York City in the United States – could lead to serious financial difficulties. It is also possible for governments to borrow so much for social capital and other purposes that insufficient funds are available for investment by the private sector in factories, mines, refineries, and other job-creating projects.

d) Students should have some understanding of how the federal government can use its taxing, spending, and borrowing powers to prevent extreme ups and downs in the Canadian economy and maintain economic stability. The way the government uses these three powers is called fiscal policy; economic stability – the goal of fiscal policy – is defined as full employment at current prices. It is apparent that when the sum total of all the goods and services wanted by Canadians (the aggregate demand) is considerably less than what the country can produce, there will be a strong depressing tendency in the economy. Factories will not be run at full capacity, men will be laid off, the national income will decline, consumption will drop still further and a downward spiral into economic recession could result. Conversely, when the aggregate demand exceeds what the country can produce when working at full capacity, prices will rise rapidly and a period of inflation may result.

Students should understand that when a recession threatens, present economic theory suggests that the federal government's fiscal policy should be designed to encourage consumption and thus stimulate the economy. The federal government can do this in several different ways. It can reduce taxes, thereby leaving more money in the hands of individuals and businesses so they can increase their own consumption. It can increase its own spending on everything from public works to increased pensions, unemployment benefits, and family allowances. Lower taxes combined with higher government spending naturally means

107

a budget deficit. In other words, expenditures will exceed revenues and the government will probably have to borrow and add to the public debt in order to cover the difference. There was a time when this kind of deficit financing was frowned on. Governments were meant to stay within their budgets, spending only what they received in tax revenues. Now it is recognized that efforts to balance the budget during a recession only make matters worse. A decline in business activity during a recession would result in a reduction in tax revenues. To maintain an annually balanced budget, the government would have to cut back on its expenditures and this would have a further depressing effect on the economy.

On the other hand, when Canada is threatened with inflation because aggregate demands exceeds supply, the government's fiscal policy should be designed to slow down consumption and prevent excessive price increases. Thus the government can increase personal and corporate income taxes, sales taxes, and other taxes, thereby taking purchasing power away from individuals and businesses and limiting their consumption. In theory the government can also cut back on its expenditures, since with more tax revenue and less spending, it would have a budget surplus. Students should understand, however, that the government's ability to cut back expenditures is limited. Many items such as interest on the public debt, many health and welfare programs, salaries and pensions for public servants are fixed in advance. The party in power in Ottawa would have a tough time trying to convince people to take salary cuts, reduced pensions or family allowances and pay more taxes when, at the same time, it was running a budget surplus. Thus it is much easier to use fiscal policies to stimulate the economy than to slow it down.

Students should understand that management of the money supply is another way in which the federal government can try to maintain stability in the Canadian economy. As a starting point, they should understand that a general shortage of money tends to cause a recession. This is because individuals and businesses find it harder and more expensive to borrow money or secure credit. Since it is difficult to get money, people will be forced to consume less; declining consumption means reduced sales, less profit, idle equipment, and lay-offs. Business will cut back on investments because sales and profits are declining and because loans for expansion cost more. Lower incomes and fewer jobs cause still further reduction in consumption, sales, profits, and so on in a downward spiral toward a serious recession. Conversely, when there is a surplus money supply, there is too much consumption, too much investment, too much competition for limited goods and services, the economy becomes overheated and threatened with inflation.

As a further introductory point, students should understand that cash in the pockets of people for their day-to-day needs is only a small part of the money supply. The most important source of money is the deposits in the nine chartered banks of Canada. The great majority of adult individuals and businesses in Canada have deposits with one or another of these banks. There is absolutely no chance that all of these people, or even a small fraction of them, will show up at the same time and ask to take all of their money out in hard cash. This being so, the banks are legally allowed to lend up to almost 90 per cent of their deposits

108

to businessmen and consumers who need money. When people borrow from a bank they usually do not walk out with currency in their pockets. Instead, the loans are simply added as book entries in the borrowers' bank accounts. In other words, the loans become additional bank deposits. The borrowers issue cheques against these accounts to pay for the goods or services they need and these cheques, in turn, end up in someone else's account. In very simplified terms this is how the chartered banks, through the deposits and loans of their customers, create "money."

Students should understand that the federal government can influence the chartered banks to increase or decrease the money supply and thereby stimulate or slow down the economy. These government activities, or monetary policies, are determined and carried out by the Bank of Canada. Despite the fact that the federal government owns the Bank of Canada, it operates autonomously and virtually free of political pressure. Only when there is a conflict of opinion between the governor and directors of the bank and the party in power can Parliament interfere. The Bank of Canada also serves as banker for the chartered banks, which gives it some control over the entire banking system.

Students should understand that the great majority of Canadians have come to accept, however reluctantly, a large amount of governmental intervention in the economic life of the country. There seems to be general agreement, at least in principle, that any civilized political community has some responsibility to the poor, the aged, the handicapped, the unemployed, and others who are unable to fend adequately for themselves; that governments also should provide social capital and related services which the market system does not produce; that governments, acting in the interests of society as a whole, should lay down some of the rules under which the private sector of the economy operates; that governments should use whatever powers they have to prevent extreme ups and downs and maintain a stable economy; and that since almost all of their activities cost money, governments should have the right to levy different kinds of taxes. But although there may be agreement in principle with all of these economic policies of government, the detailed applications of them are continuing, major sources of controversy and tension in Canada.

The nature of controversy and tension should become clearer as students understand that a great many economic decisions made by governments benefit some Canadians and adversely affect the welfare of others. There may be a loose consensus, for example, that a new airport is needed, that garbage and nuclear wastes should be safely buried, or that additional electric power should be supplied. But where do the governments build the noisy airport, erect the ugly transmission lines, or dump the garbage and contaminated wastes? The understandable answer always is anywhere but not near me.

On a much broader scale, students should understand that a great deal of government economic activity involves social costs and benefits and the need for choices affecting the lives of all Canadians. Welfare programs, for example, take money from some people and give it to others. This raises controversial questions, such as how much welfare can society support? Does the country need even more welfare or have governments already become overly protective? Are welfare payments now high enough to undermine individual initiative and the desire to work and save? Is the work ethic an out-moded concept in modern society? Is the tax burden destroying incentives to invest in the private sector? Does this kind of government intervention seriously weaken the market system and the principle of individual economic freedom or are the threats more imagined than real?

Students should understand that somewhat similar controversial questions are involved in all government efforts to provide social capital. How much social capital can the country afford? Is investment in social capital more productive in the long run than investment in the private sector? Do Canadians expect too much from governments? Are they living beyond the country's means? What economic circumstances are needed to support a growing investment in social capital? If choices must be made, what are the priorities? What kinds of social capital are most urgently needed? Are the needs the same in all parts of Canada or are there important regional differences?

Students should understand that underlying and influencing these questions is the more fundamental one of the general climate of opinion created by the kind of rules laid down by governments for the private sector of the economy. Is the private sector sufficiently regulated to be fair and provide satisfaction for the majority of Canadians? If not, what additional controls seem to be needed? Conversely, is the private sector in danger of being over-regulated and taxed so that initiative and competition are stifled? Under existing rules, is the economy growing fast enough to support the rising expectations of the people? Is rapid economic growth a valid social goal or should slower growth and a change in life-styles be encouraged? Is the public sector growing too fast? Are governments becoming too big, remote, and costly? How do salaries and pensions in the public sector compare with those in the private sector? Do governments manage their revenues and expenditures as efficiently as businesses in the private sector?

Students should understand that questions of this kind have created fundamental differences in Canadian public opinion. They should recall that some Canadians advocate more government intervention and control and an evolution to economic democracy while others are strongly in favor of as much free enterprise as possible. At present, it is probably safe to conclude that the majority of Canadians favor the mixed enterprise system and hope an appropriate balance between the private and public sectors can be achieved.

Students should understand that the management of the Canadian mixed enterprise system is an extremely complicated task. While the record of Canadian governments is better than frequently supposed, incidents of extravagance and favoritism add to the controversies associated with so many of the economic activities of governments. Students should fully understand, however, that most of the economic activities of governments have been stimulated by public expectations, that they are generally intended to bring satisfactions to as many Canadians as possible, and that up to now the mixed enterprise system has given Canada one of the highest living standards in the world.

10. Intergovernmental relations and the Canadian economy

What economic powers are held by each of the three levels of government in

Canada and what possible sources of conflict exist as a result of this distribution of power?

What specific evidence suggests that federal–provincial confrontations are primarily over economic issues?

What are the minimum powers the federal government should have in order to keep the Canadian economy operating in the interests of Canadian society as a whole?

a) Before tackling this very important topic, students should carefully review the understandings they have developed about federal–provincial relations in Canada (see Chapter 5, Section 8, on intergovernmental relations).

Against this background, students should understand that in Canada's mixed enterprise system, where the range of economic activities by governments is so extensive and their costs so high, the great majority of intergovernmental confrontations are caused by economic questions. According to the constitutional division of powers, the federal government, in addition to many other things, has exclusive jurisdiction over the public debt, the regulation of trade and commerce, the raising of money by any form of taxation or borrowing, banking, currency, coinage, and the issue of paper money. In general terms, it is these powers that allow the federal government, using various fiscal and monetary policies, to manage the economy and attempt to achieve the national economic goals of full employment, stability, continued growth, and so on.

Students should understand that the constitution gives the provinces exclusive jurisdiction over "all matters of a merely local or private nature" within each province. Among other things, these include the management and sale of all public lands, local public works, property and civil rights, direct taxation and borrowing on the sole credit of the province, education, municipal institutions, hospitals and all forms of charity. In 1867 the exercise of these powers was not expected to cost the provinces very much money. Since then, public works such as the building of hospitals and schools, the construction of roads and superhighways, the care of the poor and handicapped, the development of hydroelectric power facilities, financial aid to the municipalities for sewage disposal, water supplies, and urban transit facilities, and many other modern developments, have placed tremendously heavy financial burdens on the provinces and their municipalities. Although the provincial and municipal governments combined now spend more than the federal government, the expenditures of the authorities in Ottawa also have sky-rocketed. Thus, with expenditures escalating at all three levels of government, it is natural that one of the most contentious issues at federal–provincial conferences is the distribution of taxing powers and revenues.

Students should understand, therefore, that in the Canadian political community it is inevitable that there will be a certain amount of overlapping taxation and conflict between the federal and provincial governments over tax-sharing agreements. At all major federal–provincial conferences, some of the provinces almost invariably will demand more tax room, meaning that they want a larger share of personal and corporate income taxes. Faced with escalating expenditures also, the federal government naturally will resist these demands as vigorously as possible. In doing so, the federal government sometimes is supported by

111

the have-not provinces, which benefit from federal equalization payments. Indirectly, the municipalities contribute to the pressures at federal–provincial conferences. Property taxes (over which they have exclusive control) simply will not cover the expenditures needed to run modern towns and cities; so they are continually pressing their provincial governments for financial aid and this is reflected in the demands of the provinces at conferences with the federal government.

Students should understand that federal spending is a very controversial issue in Canada. Until recently, the federal government has had a large number of complex cost-sharing and conditional grant agreements with the provinces. Although their use is now declining, cost-sharing plans and grants made on the condition that the provinces do certain things have led to an intrusion on provincial rights by the federal government. Thus, major cost-sharing agreements such as medical care, hospital insurance, and post-secondary education have led to federal intervention in welfare services, education, and other matters that are constitutionally under the jurisdiction of the provinces. These programs, combined with equalization payments and all the other efforts of the federal government to alleviate regional economic disparities, have been deeply resented by some provinces and forced them, so the argument goes, to follow the priorities of the federal government rather than their own.

Students should understand that in recent years the federal government has yielded time after time to provincial demands extending over a progressively wider range of economic matters. In these federal–provincial confrontations some of the provinces are strengthened by certain other constitutional economic provisions. Considering the importance of the resource-based industries in Canada, for example, and the fact that natural resources fall under provincial jurisdiction through property and civil rights and the management of public lands, it is understandable that some provinces are now economically very powerful. Politicians from these provinces bargain with Ottawa knowing that they have the advantage of wealth, popular support, well-financed party campaign funds, and a highly trained bureaucracy. In summary, students should understand that the provinces, using federal–provincial conferences as their main instrument, have eroded many federal constitutional powers and that the Canadian system of government is more decentralized than ever before.

b) Students should understand that all the preceding considerations raise the question of how much more decentralization Canadian federalism can withstand. What are the minimum powers required by the federal government to manage the economy and achieve its national goals? Are its goals valid any longer? Does the country need to rethink its economic and social objectives and try to find new ones that might sustain the minimum levels of consensus needed for a viable federalism? Is it possible to manage such a vast and regionally diverse country with centralized fiscal and monetary policies? Should the constitution be scrapped and a fresh start made or is the present one flexible enough to satisfy the legitimate aspirations of the provinces? Can constitutional adjustments eliminate federal–provincial confrontations or are such things absolutely inevitable in any federally structured society?

Students should understand that in the continuing process of federal–provincial bargaining, there are only a few essential powers that the central government must retain in order to have effective control over the national economy. These would include control over national defence, most aspects of foreign policy, international and interprovincial trade, the Bank of Canada and monetary policy, and sufficient tax revenues to service the public debt, cover the operating costs of the government, and provide adequate equalization payments to the have-not provinces. With these powers and possibly some control over the administration of justice and human rights, the central government would have at least the minimum jurisdiction required by a modern, industrialized nation. Students should understand that beyond these few essential federal powers, everything else (and this includes a great deal) is open to negotiation. It is quite possible for the provinces to have more authority to make their own decisions about health, welfare, communications, language, culture, education, natural resources, and many other matters.

Students should recall that controversy and tension are not only inevitable in all societies but, within broad limits, are also constructive forces. At times tensions can rise to dangerously high levels and possibly become destructive. Whether Canada is approaching this point is debatable. There can be little doubt, however, that current conditions present Canadians with a stressful but creative opportunity to mould a new future together. This will require outstanding leadership and an informed, supportive public opinion capable of handling tension with understanding, political skill, and wisdom. These requirements place a heavy responsibility on the media and the schools. It is interesting to speculate whether these two important socializing agencies have the capacity to meet the present challenges of Canadian federalism. If the trend toward decentralization continues, the need for Canadians to better understand each other becomes even greater. Will the ten provincial departments of education develop more effective cooperative procedures and encourage the schools sometimes to transcend provincial and regional concerns with a counterbalancing pan-Canadian vision?

B. HISTORICAL ANALYSIS

This set of questions provides a general framework for a fairly straightforward economic history of Canada from 1867 to 1975.

11. *At the time of Confederation, what were the most significant differences in the structure and functioning of the Canadian economy compared to the present?*

In 1867 what early signs of contemporary economic life in Canada were apparent?

What new technologies were becoming important and were these to be detrimental or beneficial to Canada during the last half of the nineteenth century?

What were the main economic concerns of the federal government during the first few years following Confederation and how important was the government's role in the Canadian economy?

12. *What was the National Policy, why was it introduced, and how was it designed to develop a transcontinental economy in Canada?*

To what extent did the National Policy attempt to strengthen "artificial" east–west boundary lines and to what extent was it simply an extension of historical trends?

What North American and world conditions prevented the National Policy from working as planned during the remaining years of the nineteenth century? What effects did this failure have on dominion–provincial relations and how were these compounded by racial and religious issues?

What alternatives to the National Policy were offered to the electorate in the federal elections of 1887, 1891, and 1896, and what were the results in each case?

13. *What changing North American and world conditions during the early years of the twentieth century favored Canada and insured the success of the National Policy? In particular, what new technologies were especially suited to Canada's resource base?*

What policies were introduced by the federal government to supplement favorable international trends and to enhance Canada's prosperity? In particular, what major economic undertakings were encouraged by the government of Canada and for what special reasons were they encouraged?

What sectors of the economy and what parts of Canada benefited most from the prosperity of these years?

Why did the economic development of Canada during the first years of the twentieth century lead to another movement for reciprocity with the United States and what happened to this issue? Why were so many American branch plants established in Canada in this period and what government policies encouraged this growth?

14. *In what ways did Canada's particular economic contribution to the Allied Powers during the First World War make it more difficult to adjust to a peacetime economy after 1918? How did Canada's position in this respect differ from the United States?*

What new technologies, invented or expanded during the First World War, began to change the economic structure of Canada and the life-styles of Canadians? Of the new technologies, which one had the most far-reaching consequences? What were the most significant changes in society resulting from the new technologies?

Despite the obvious prosperity of the late 1920s, what basic weaknesses existed in the economies of Canada and the other industrialized countries? To what extent were these weaknesses compounded by economic problems arising from the war and the peace settlements?

15. *What were the causes of the 1929 crash and subsequent depression and why was it more severe than any previous depression?*

In what ways was Canada particularly exposed to the impact of the Great Depression? What sectors of the economy, what parts of the country, and what groups of people were especially hard hit by the Depression?

114

What were the major remedial measures adopted by Canada and other countries and how effective were these measures? In the long run what were the main reasons for the industrialized countries pulling out of the Great Depression?

What lessons were learned as a result of the Depression and how did these eventually affect the structure and functioning of the entire Candian economy?

16. *What new technologies, invented or expanded during the Second World War, greatly changed the Canadian economy and the life-styles of Canadians? Of the new technologies, which ones have had the most far-reaching consequences and to what extent have these been beneficial to mankind?*

What political and economic reasons made it easier for Canada to adjust to a peacetime economy after 1945?

What features of the present-day Canadian economy began to appear shortly after the end of the Second World War?

What sectors of the economy and what parts of the country benefited most from the new technologies and the post-1945 economic boom? What new resources were discovered that greatly enhanced the postwar boom in Canada and added to the strength of her economy?

At what times and for what reasons has Canada experienced an economic slow-down from 1945 to the present? Why were none of these recessions as serious as the Great Depression of the 1930s? What measures did the federal government introduce to counter these recessions and how effective were they?

17. *What evidence can be used to show that economic growth in Canada and elsewhere has been increasing exponentially in recent years?*

What are the major reasons for this rapid increase in the pace of change?

What are some of the most serious questions raised for Canadians by exponential growth rates in the economy?

To what extent is the Canadian economy and the federal structure of society and government capable of handling these questions?

C. FUTURE ANALYSIS

18. *Assuming the continuation of present trends, what predictions may be made about each of the major features of the Canadian economy?*

Are all of the present trends in the best interests of Canadian society? If not, which ones should be redirected, what policies will be needed to achieve this purpose, and what might be the results of these policies?

19. *What are the most important of the problems that Canada and other countries will face in the future as a result of man's increasing technological power to master nature?*

Will technological developments continue to solve the problems created by technology or will fundamental changes in attitudes and life-styles be required in the future?

20. *What are some of the great imponderables that make all predictions about the economic future so uncertain? What might Canadians and other peoples of the world do to reduce the uncertainties caused by these imponderables?*

D.   AN ALTERNATIVE APPROACH TO CANADIAN ECONOMIC HISTORY

Another approach to an historical analysis of the Canadian economic system is provided by an hypothesis with great possibilities as a unifying theme for a study of the changing structure and functioning of the Canadian economy. Of course, as an hypothesis, it may or may not stand up to the evidence. Nevertheless, testing the hypothesis could be a most interesting and rewarding study.

The hypothesis is as follows. During the past one hundred or so years, very important technological developments have appeared in certain clearly defined periods of time. These new technologies and the reasons for their appearance at specific intervals in the past can be readily identified. In turn, the new technologies have substantially changed every aspect of the Canadian economy (as well as, of course, the economies of most other industrialized countries). Thus, it can be maintained that the basic forces shaping the economic system and influencing economic decision-making all stem from periods of technological changes and their impact on the Canadian environment. The following questions have been designed to provide a format for considering Canada's economic history in this less conventional way.

1. *At what times in the Canadian past have there been periods of comparatively rapid technological innovation and change?*

In each period, what were the most important of the new technologies, where did they originate, and what factors caused their development at this particular time and place?

2. *How did the new technologies appearing in each time period eventually affect the following features of the Canadian economy:*
- *the structure and relative importance of different sectors of the economy?*
- *the organization, functions, and powers of the major economic groups in the economy?*
- *regional economic growth and, conversely, regional economic disparities?*
- *patterns of foreign trade and trade policies?*
- *economic relations with the United States?*
- *the size, organization, and methods of labor unions?*
- *the structure and functioning of business, including the growth of multinational corporations?*
- *the roles of governments and modifications in the free enterprise system?*
- *business cycles and the stability of the Canadian economy?*
- *the life-styles and living standards of Canadians?*

3. *How did the new technologies in each time period eventually affect the following:*
- *the relative economic responsibilities, power, and influence of the provinces and the federal government?*

116

– *the techniques, subject matter, and degree of stress in federal–provincial relations?*
– *the decision-making processes in both the federal and provincial levels of government?*
– *the type of economic demands (the public issues) made on the political system, the resulting political activities, and the response of governments to these demands and activities?*

4. *What is meant by the phrase "post-industrial society" and to what extent is this type of society a product of new technologies?*

To what extent have new technologies contributed to exponential growth rates in the Canadian economy?

CHAPTER VII

Studying Public Issues in Canada

The civic education program described in preceding chapters provides opportunities (over a period of several years) for students to develop a large number of understandings about the nature and functioning of the Canadian political community. All of these understandings can be greatly enhanced through the study of public issues. Indeed, with skilful teaching, they will remain with students long after the details of particular issues are forgotten, providing them with a fundamental framework of ideas that will be useful regardless of what specific public issues they might be required to consider in the future.

This study of public issues is designed for senior high school students; it should be the climax to all their preceding work in Canada studies. This being so, it would be unfortunate if public issues were studied in isolation. Every effort should be made to ensure that this final part of civic education is used not only to help students know about the issues but also to review and internalize the major understandings about the Canadian political community they have acquired in previous years.

It is of paramount importance that students keep in mind the cause-and-effect relationships of the basic features of Canada which are involved in any nation-wide public issue. The basic features of Canada not only help to generate the issues themselves but also impose constraints on political leadership and set broad limits within which the decision-making processes take place. Any major decision, in turn, affects the environment either by resolving the problem and lessening social stress, or by unsatisfactory ad hoc compromises that prompt new demands.

It is important, therefore, that teachers should help students to develop the ability to think about public issues in terms of the circular cause–effect–cause relationships between the environment, the structure of the political and economic systems, and the decision-making processes in Canada.

The analysis of public issues provides opportunities to study public opinions in a political democracy. The strongest feelings, attitudes, and values of Canadians are first formed by many local, immediate forces based on family, religion, ethnicity, language, place of residence, and other factors. The tremendous variety of these forces produces a corresponding, almost infinite variety of feelings and attitudes toward all major public issues in Canada. When analysing public issues, therefore, students should look for concrete evidence of differing viewpoints and the reasons for them. In this way, they might develop a deeper appreciation of the feelings, attitudes, and outlooks of other Canadians from different regions and backgrounds.

Public opinions in a democracy like Canada are formed partly by the mass media. Some of the questions raised in Chapter 5 about the role of the media should be used in the study of public issues so that students can evaluate the influence of the media on specific public opinions. The application of these questions to particular issues should help students to extent their understandings of opinion formation and the powers and quality of the media in Canada.

Political parties also help to mould public opinions. National political parties are often regarded as unifying influences in Canada. The study of public issues provides ample opportunities to test this hypothesis. A careful analysis of federal and provincial party politics on any major issue should help students to decide whether political parties are in fact serving the interests of the country as a whole or whether they are divisive influences.

The study of public issues provides opportunities to learn more about the political culture and behavior of Canadians and how they react to any important national concern. Do Canadians appear to be interested in the issue? How is this interest expressed? Are some groups more involved than others and, if so, why? Does the Canadian public appear to be well or poorly informed on the issue? Is the issue receiving the attention it merits? Are other issues of more concern to groups of Canadians and, if so, does this represent a lack of perspective on what is important? Questions of this kind should help students to increase their understanding of the quality of public life in Canada.

National issues can be roughly classified not only by their degree of importance but also by their general nature. Most public issues seem to be directly or indirectly associated with economics and material well-being; issues that appear on the surface to be primarily concerned with language, culture, or the quality of the natural environment, for example, may be found on closer analysis to have strong economic undertones. The economic aspects of any issue may involve both immediate bread-and-butter considerations and long-term ones that require foresight in forming an opinion. When analysing a public issue, students should try to identify the economic components and estimate the extent to which various groups are preoccupied with immediate material gains. This should help students not only to further understand the nature of public opinions but also the degree to which ad hoc or long-term considerations influence the decision-making process.

The study of public issues provides the best possible opportunity to observe interest groups in action. Virtually every public issue, by very definition, will involve contending interest groups. When analysing public issues, students should identify the interest groups involved, their motives, their weaknesses and sources

120

of power, their methods of influencing the public, the media, and the decision-makers, and where possible, their degree of success. In doing so, students also should observe the existence of weak, unorganized groups who may have a stake in the issue but have practically no way of expressing it. This approach to public issues should help students not only to understand the importance of interest groups but also the need for governments to assess all the costs and benefits involved in the attempt to find satisfactory solutions.

The study of public issues should help students to understand more about the decision-making processes in Canada. Among the great many questions that might be used, the following will give some indication of the general direction that this kind of analysis should take. How was this issue raised in the first place; did government take the initiative or did it simply respond to public demand? (Where, for example, did the decision to have Canada adopt the metric system originate?) Did this particular problem become on election issue and if so, to what extent did the outcome of the election influence the decision made? Were strong regional viewpoints involved and was the decision of obvious benefit to some parts of Canada, or did the issue, perhaps in different forms, persist? What effects did the decision have on tension levels in Canada? In the final analysis, was the decision made democratically or by the elites? Is there evidence to suggest that Canadians tend to leave certain issues to the experts, and if so, what kind of issues? In retrospect, do some apparently democratic and popular decisions seem to have been unwise, or has the majority always been right? Whatever questions are used, they should be designed to help students understand as fully as possible the strengths and weaknesses of democracy in Canada.

When a society is faced with a problem, choices or alternative courses of action remain open for only a limited period of time. For a number of reasons that students should identify through their studies of public issues, the solution to a problem may be postponed too long; attitudes and interests then have time to polarize and harden so that the range of alternatives is gradually reduced. Bargaining from rigid positions within a very narrow range of choices invariably increases tension, creates a crisis atmosphere, and makes a democratic compromise exceedingly difficult. This process can continue until opportunities for choice and compromise disappear entirely and a society loses the power to control some part of its future. By testing this hypothesis during the study of public issues, students should gain further insights into the ability of Canadian citizens and institutions to resolve conflict before tension levels become dangerously high.

In the study of public issues, students should also be encouraged to turn their attention beyond the confines of their own country. Many issues of great importance to Canadians are merely symptoms of world-wide problems whose magnitude transcends geographic boundaries. Some of our most cherished personal, regional, or national goals could be frustrated by global trends over which Canada has but limited control. In a world becoming more interdependent, Canadians cannot afford to be too preoccupied with their own internal affairs. Students, as future citizens and decision-makers, simply must understand the significances of the major issues facing mankind and the demands these will make on Canada.

Finally, it should be observed that the study of public issues provides opportunities for teachers to help students acquire several very important intellectual skills.

Long-term considerations are involved in most public issues. Decisions made today almost inevitably will have consequences far into the future; some decisions, once taken, are virtually incapable of being reversed. The construction of the Churchill Dam in Labrador and the flooding of millions of acres of land under fifty feet of water is an obvious example of a decision whose effects will last for generations. The extraction and transportation of Arctic oil and gas, the development of the James Bay Project, the disposal of nuclear wastes, the reconstruction of any city's downtown core, the building of access roads to wilderness areas, are among the many public issues that could be used to illustrate the long-term results of most policy decisions. It could be easily maintained that a society which makes its decisions on ad hoc immediate considerations or cannot agree on long-term policies is behaving unwisely. One of the most important intellectual skills teachers can help students to develop is foresight, the ability to weigh alternatives in terms of future costs and benefits.

With increasing interdependence both within and between political communities, space also becomes an important factor when considering public issues. Any significant decision made in one part of Canada by either governments or a major economic group is likely to have consequences in other parts of the country and possibly abroad. More importantly for such an exposed country as Canada, events or decisions in distant places directly affect the lives of Canadians. Thus, oil policies determined in Venezuela or the Middle East affect the fuel supplies of all eastern Canada. Crop failures in Florida, Brazil, Russia, or elsewhere, atomic testing in the atmosphere by the newer nuclear powers, the internal economic or political difficulties of one nation in a trading group – all of these have a ripple effect throughout the world and directly or indirectly influence life in Canada. Regional and world-wide interdependence, particularly in economic and environmental concerns, indicates that another intellectual skill teachers should help students to acquire is the ability to think in terms of international causes and consequences.

Public issues can only be viewed intelligently within historical perspectives. Almost any current Canadian problem is a product of the basic features of Canada, is fairly deeply rooted in the past, and can be thoroughly understood only in the light of what has already happened. Attitudes toward American investment developed in a vacuum of present considerations only might be changed by understanding that previous Canadian policies deliberately encouraged the establishment of branch plants in this country. Similarly, the causes of the indifference of people in various regions of Canada to one another's problems and the open hostility between some of them undoubtedly could be softened by a deeper appreciation of the historical and geographic roots of regional differences. Or again, wage and profit expectations in resource industries might be modified by an understanding of the historic role of these industries, their need to remain competitive in foreign markets, and their significance in the total Canadian economy. Accordingly, another important intellectual skill which teachers should help students to develop is the ability to think historically, always to view current problems from the perspectives of the past.

PROBLEM AREAS OF CONTINUING CONCERN TO CANADIANS

This section concludes with six important areas of concern to Canadians and puts forth some major headings which can be used in the study of each one. An area of concern should be treated as an integrated whole. Individual public issues should be regarded simply as components of an overall area of concern, and only in exceptional cases should an individual public issue receive separate and exclusive study. The objective should be to help students acquire an overview of each area of concern.

Areas of concern tend to be permanent factors in Canadian society; likewise, most of the issues arising in each area of concern tend to persist over fairly long periods of time. The immediate manifestations of a public issue, however, will vary greatly. For example, native rights is a persistent issue in Canada· which at the present moment attracts public attention through immediate events such as the James Bay development, the northen pipeline discussions, the pollution of the fish in the English River, or confrontation in Kenora. These temporary manifestations of any issue should be used only for illustrative purposes and not as topics for detailed investigation.

The sets of questions which follow should be used to study each area of concern. It is not suggested, however, that all of the public issues indicated by the sub-headings should be included. A selection of these, made according to local considerations, should be sufficient to give students an adequate knowledge and understanding of each general area of concern.

The questions have been worded to apply to a specific, individual issue. However, with slight modifications they can be used equally well for a general area of concern and a series of interrelated problems. The questions are not intended to be followed in fixed sequence, but are designed to form a total package for studying any major public issue in Canada. Furthermore, some teachers may prefer to start with the historical rather than with the contemporary questions. In any case, it is important for students to become interested and motivated by sensing from the outset the significance of the issue in question.

A.   CONTEMPORARY ANALYSIS

1. *What is the real issue or point of controversy?*

Why is it an issue?

To what extent is this issue the product of the interaction of the five basic features of Canada?

What evidence of the existence of this issue can be identified both locally and in other regions of Canada?

What are the most significant questions raised by this issue?

2. *How did this issue most recently enter into or become a part of public opinion in Canada?*

What kinds of political activity is this issue stimulating?

123

What are the similarities and differences of viewpoint among Canadians on this issue?

What degree of tension has been created by this issue and what are its effects on the Canadian political community?

B. HISTORICAL ANALYSIS

3. *When did this issue first become apparent and what specific circumstances caused its appearance?*

To what extent were these circumstances the product of the five basic features of Canada?

What kinds of political activity, what controversies and tensions, what decisions resulted from the first appearance of this issue?

What were the results of this political activity? To what extent did the issue and the need for further political activity persist?

How did the strengths and weaknesses of the Canadian political system influence this outcome?

4. *At what subsequent times has this issue become of significant concern to Canadians?*

What circumstances or conditions prompted renewed interest in this issue each time? Did the resulting political activities differ from the previous time the issue was raised?

What were the results of political activity each time? To what extent did the problem and the need for further political activity persist?

How did the strengths and weaknesses of the Canadian political system influence the results in each case?

5. *Why did this issue persist throughout the Canadian past? Were mistakes in decisions made in the past, and if so, what other choices might have been made?*

In what ways has the contemporary issue grown from the previous experiences of the Canadian political community? Do historical developments hinder or aid attempts to find solutions?

C. FUTURE ANALYSIS

6. *What choices are now open to Canadians when dealing with this issue?*

Which choice appears to be best for Canadians and their political community, and what evidence from the past and present can be used to justify it?

On the basis of past experiences, what qualities might help Canadians to deal with this issue in as constructive a way as possible?

What trends may be predicted in this issue? In what ways will these trends affect the structure and functioning of the political system?

I. Technology and industrialization in Canada

(a) Resource use and conservation in Canada; the special area of energy.

(b) Waste disposal and protection of the environment.

(c) Urban concentration and the problems of the cities.

(d) Rural poverty and decay; regional economic disparities.

(e) The increasing need for recreational facilities; recreational land use and policies.

(f) Concentrations of power; big business, unions, and government.

(g) Economic instability; unemployment and inflation.

(h) The creation of new human wants and demands; the development of an affluent, consumption-oriented society.

(i) The complexity of policy decisions, effects on political processes and the democratic control of society; faith in technological omnipotence.

II. Biculturalism in a multi-ethnic Canada

(a) Major ethnic groups in Canada; ethnic and cultural cooperation or discrimination in Canada; the reality or mythology of the Canadian mosaic; the costs and benefits of multiculturalism.

(b) The concentration of the francophone population in the province of Quebec; distinctive characteristics of French-Canadian culture; perceived and real threats to the survival of French-Canadian culture in Quebec.

(c) Francophone minorities in other parts of Canada, the relationships of these minorities with Quebeckers and with English-speaking Canadians; English-speaking minorities in Quebec; the relationships of these minorities with the French-Canadian majority and with English-speaking Canadians elsewhere.

(d) Party politics in Quebec since the Quiet Revolution of the 1960s; the separatist movement, the rise to power of the Parti Québecois; the official positions taken by the government of Quebec at recent federal–provincial conferences; the attitudes and behavior of English-speaking Canadians to all of these developments.

(e) The degree of participation by Quebeckers in national political, economic, and cultural organizations; the extent of official and personal contacts between English- and French-speaking Canadians.

(f) The role of the media in Quebec and in other parts of the country in fostering understanding or misunderstanding between the two main linguistic groups in Canada.

(g) The relationships between bilingualism/biculturalism and multiculturalism and their effects on national policies.

(h) A summary evaluation of the prospects for federalism in a bilingual, multi-ethnic country where one cultural group forms a substantial majority in one province but occupies minority positions elsewhere.

125

III. Canada's relations with the United States

(a) Exposure to American cultural influences; the particular case of American influence on all levels of education in Canada; the various media through which Canadians are influenced by American culture; efforts by Canadians to offset external cultural influences and the effectiveness of these measures.

(b) Economic influences of the United States; the operation in Canada of American-owned multinational corporations; American-based international labor unions; balance of payments between Canada and the United States; efforts by Canadians to offset some of the adverse economic influences of the United States and the effectiveness of these measures.

(c) Political influences of the United States; the relationship between economic power and the possibility of political influence; techniques for exerting pressure; actual and potential areas of friction between the two countries; military ties with the United States and their consequences for Canada.

IV. The quality of life in Canada

(a) Evidence of changing values, attitudes, and behavior among Canadians; reasons for these changes and the desirability or otherwise of current trends.

(b) Standards of living in Canada; class structure and mobility; health and welfare programs, their cost and benefits, and the various attitudes of Canadians toward these programs.

(c) Cultural opportunities and the quality of cultural life in Canada; education and the development or waste of human resources; the quality and influences of the mass media and advertising.

(d) Urban living in Canada; current trends in city living; the quality of life in smaller centres and in rural Canada.

(e) The protection of human rights in Canada; the quality of the legal system; freedom and authority in Canada; the special case of the native peoples; the extent to which the basic premises of a democratic society are willingly supported by Canadians.

V. The adequacy of the Canadian political system

(*Note:* this area of concern overlaps some aspects of the preceding ones and will serve to a large extent as a review.)

(a) The degree of support given by Canadians to their political community; more specifically, the degree of support given to the political regime; an estimate of whether this support is sufficient to sustain the Canadian political community.

(b) The capacity of the population and the political system to adjust to and and lessen the strains caused by the federal structure of Canadian society.

(c) The capacity of the population and the political system to control the impact of technology and industrialization in all of their more important manifestations.

(d) The quality of political leadership in Canada and the responses of Canadians to leadership; present trends in the political decision-making process and their likely effects on the Canadian political community.

(e) The apparent preoccupation of federal political parties with survival, "national unity," and a "Canadian identity," and the effects of this concern on efforts to establish other mutually acceptable goals.

(f) Public opinion in Canada and the effects on Canadian federalism of such things as the mass media, education, political parties, the electoral process, regional and ethnic loyalties and prejudices, external political, economic, and cultural influences.

VI. Global issues and Canada's external policies

(a) Exponential growth rates in a world of finite resources; man's technological power to master nature and his use of this power; consumption of non-renewable resources; population growth; world food supplies; the special case of energy and the imbalanced economies of countries relying on imported oil; environmental protection and the disposal of human and industrial wastes.

(b) Nuclear technology; its non-military advantages and dangers; nuclear weapons, the continuing escalation of the arms race and the persistence of balance of terror strategies; the trade in sophisticated weaponry by industrialized nations with developing countries.

(c) The existence of two main contending groups of nations and the reasons for their rivalries; the efforts on a global scale of both the East and the West to influence the Third World countries; internal and external tensions within Third World countries in Africa, the Middle East, Asia, and South America.

(d) The gap between the rich and poor nations; the contrast between the industrialized, affluent, and consumption-oriented societies and the poverty-stricken, hungry, and survival-oriented societies; the proportion of world resources used by the industrialized nations; rising expectations among the peoples of the Third World.

(e) The failure of the major industrialized powers to resolve the twin problems of inflation and unemployment; imbalances in world trade and international payments; adverse conditions and the growth of economic nationalism; evidence of internal stress and severe discontents in some of the industrialized countries.

(f) Canadian foreign policies and the attitudes of Canadians on global issues; aid to selected poor countries; immigration policies related to people from overcrowded, underdeveloped areas and political refugees; world food supplies and the use of Canada's surplus farm products; economic nationalism and Canada's relations with her major trading partners; Canadian positions at international conferences convened to consider global economic, environmental, and other issues.

(g) The main international organizations through which Canada's foreign policies are expressed; membership and roles in the Commonwealth, the United Nations, and other non-military organizations; membership and roles in international military organizations; the use of Canada's forces in peacekeeping assignments; the costs and benefits of current Canadian commitments to all these various international organizations; the interest and attitudes of Canadians toward these commitments.

(h) The close relationships between domestic affairs and foreign policy; the difficulties in external affairs created by the federal structure of Canadian society; questions of jurisdiction in external relations between the provinces and the federal government; the prospects for Canadians to find acceptable national goals in the general area of foreign policy; and the question of whether Canadians are preoccupied with purely domestic concerns.

Epilogue

Until recently, it was possible for most young women and men to graduate from secondary schools in Canada confident that the future was theirs for the taking and that they had a clear path to their own selected goals in life. That era has passed. It has been replaced by one of rapid change and great uncertainties, where the future can no longer be taken for granted. It is easy to paint a dark picture of the world our students will be entering in the 1980s; but in this epilogue we also try to point to some highlights and potential bright spots that seem to offer real hope for the future.

The most important goals in life are associated with the drive within all of us for personal happiness, security, affection, and the achievement of feelings of individual worth, dignity and freedom. The pursuit of these goals is the toughest task of life. Our greatest joys and deepest heartaches arise in this area of intimate human relations; yet personal goals can never be sought in isolation but always in and through society. Society today has the power to undermine, to frustrate, and even to destroy the most carefully planned lifetime objectives.

We are living in the most revolutionary era in history. After centuries of painfully slow growth, the world has suddenly exploded into a period of abnormally rapid growth. The dynamics behind this pace of change is the tremendous increase in man's scientific knowledge and his resulting awesome technological power to master any aspect of nature. Some fear this power, claiming that growth must be limited or eliminated if man is to get off his present suicidal course. Others scoff at the prophets of doom and gloom, believing that technology has the power to resolve man's problems forever. However we may feel about this debate, there can be little doubt that it has now become a fundamental human dialogue.

Involved in this dialogue is the knowledge of all the benefits that science has brought to those of us who live in industrial countries. We no longer fear the unknown, as our ancestors did, because it has been conquered. The burden of

129

excessive toil has been lifted from most of us. Many dread diseases have been eliminated. We live in material comfort beyond the wildest dreams of our grand-parents. We have leisure and freedom men have sought for centuries. In the future we will need more, not less, technology.

Involved in this dialogue also is the fear that technology could become a new dehumanizing religion. We could place too much faith in its power. Technology could become the master and not the servant of man. Already technology has given us the power, for good or ill, to do whatever we wish with nature, to consume the earth's resources at ever-increasing rates, and has raised the question of how long this growth can be sustained with resources that are finite and non-renewable.

It is important to remember also that the benefits of science are not enjoyed by the great majority of the world's population. We live in a world where too few of us consume far too much. We live in affluent societies while the remaining two-thirds of the world's population struggle for survival, constantly facing malnutrition or outright starvation. The rising expectations of the increasing millions of people in the Third World who have so little to lose poses one of the most serious questions for the industrialized nations, carrying with it as it does the prospect of violent confrontations.

World problems of this magnitude in the final analysis must be regarded as more important than our purely Canadian concerns. And yet we know that each of us needs a home base, a familiar starting place for all we do in life. That place is provided by the political community called Canada – a country for which most of us probably have a deep but seldom articulated affection. Ours is a very beautiful and richly endowed land. We are among the most fortunate people on earth; yet here, too, it would be unrealistic not to recognize that we are in danger of throwing away our opportunities, our advantages, our national endowment and our historic heritage.

The severe problems of our troubled economy are all too familiar to us. They are, however, but symptoms of a deeper malaise. We have taken too literally the prediction that the twentieth century belonged to Canada and that our resources would last forever. With a casual optimism that is only now beginning to disappear, all of us – business and labor leaders, professional people, politicians, Canadians generally – have assumed that our standards of living would continue to rise indefinitely; that a home, two cars, a boat and trailer, a summer cottage, a luxurious grocery basket, and security from cradle to grave were a normal part of life or were at least attainable.

Until recently, we have blithely taken for granted that Canada could easily maintain her position as one of the world's great trading nations. Only now are we beginning to realize that newly industrialized nations are providing tough competition and that Third World countries, also rich in many of the same natural resources as Canada, are entering their own mining boom, with government-owned exporting agencies frequently indifferent to the dangers of world surpluses. In a struggling world economy, we can no longer expect that our trading partners will yield to our complaints and grant us special favors.

Furthermore, we Canadians seem to have become a strangely timid people. Whenever we seek something in life, we turn with increasing frequency to govern-

130

ments for help. Through our demands and our excessive expectations, we have created huge, costly, rigid bureaucracies. We have enormously extended the range of government activities and we have spawned big remote governments capable of intervening in our lives at any time and in almost any way. In other words, we may be creating institutions that could destroy the freedom they were designed to protect.

Like people in other countries, Canadians face problems so complex and technical that they appear to be beyond the comprehension of most citizens. Research indicates that this helps to account for the feeling of apathy, alienation, frustration, and general indifference to long-term policies and hence to a preoccupation throughout society with immediate, self-centred issues and the fun culture. Yet people in Canada have the right to vote and within broad limits to say what they wish and to make whatever choices they want. This is a real dilemma. We believe in democracy – we must because at the moment there appears to be no other alternative – and yet we are in danger of having our futures determined by the sheer weight of numbers, by day-by-day expediency measures designed to gratify short-sighted interests. Such a society is unlikely ever to agree on common, long-term goals; yet our world is crying out for the wisest kind of long-range planning.

Our difficulties are now greatly compounded by the fact that Canadian federation, always a very delicately balanced mechanism, is more seriously threatened than ever before. In 1968, as a result of observing what the schools across Canada were teaching young people about their own country, the author of *What Culture? What Heritage?* predicted precisely the situation that now exists with the increasing alienation of Quebec and other regions of the country. The prediction was made to encourage our educators to break out of their provincial cocoons and see the national needs; it was hoped they would realize that the schools might help to meet these needs by eliminating some of the abysmal ignorance and misunderstanding that exists between people from different regions and differing linguistic, ethnic, and cultural backgrounds. It is apparent that this challenge has not yet been faced. But let us not dwell on this sad aspect of the Canadian experiment. Whatever immediate solutions may be found, we can be sure that relations between the provinces and the federal government, and among the provinces, will remain strained for years to come.

This is a dark-toned, sombre sketch of our world. We would be doing a great disservice to students to pretend these problems did not exist. We can no longer afford to over-emphasize, as we have tended to do in our schools, the principle of self-realization and fulfilment as a prime educational goal. Man is not a solitary animal. As long as social life survives, self-fulfilment is not a completely satisfactory ethical principle. The kind of Canadian and world community in which students will be living must be revealed to them in all its stark realities. Perhaps only by a frank recognition that mankind faces many harsh alternatives will our young people be able to find themselves in the world of the future.

There is a grave danger here, of course, that undue attention to problems and difficulties could alienate many students. Without a skilful blend of realistic but constructive teaching in our schools, young people could experience unnecessary anxieties and develop feelings of hopelessness or cynicism. Indeed, there is ample evidence to indicate that this is happening with some of them. Nor should we

131

over-emphasize the importance of change. An unfortunate but prevalent argument has been that, because the pace of change is so rapid, knowledge is outdated almost before it is learned and that it really does not matter what is taught. This has resulted in a severe down-grading of content and knowledge and an inordinate amount of time spent on skills to help students adjust to change without considering what standards might be used to judge the desirability of change. Young people will need all the background knowledge and intellectual skills they can get, not only to make wise decisions but also to keep up to date as the contemporary world changes.

All of the great national and international problems we have been describing in broad sweeping generalities, when analysed come down to how individuals, you and I and everyone else, think and feel and act. These qualities in us are partially determined by external stimuli. We are shaped by our environment. It is possible, therefore, to believe that the compulsions, the pressures, and the imperatives of the world we are creating will impel men and women to make lasting and beneficial changes in their attitudes, their value systems, and their priorities.

The fundamental thesis of this book is that the schools are an integral and vitally important part of the environment and that they should feel and reflect its compulsions and imperatives more sensitively than any other social agency. If we wait for necessity to compel changes in human behavior, if we drift with the times and react only when events are upon us, it may be too late. The schools must adopt a role of anticipating developments and leading society not by prescription, not by advocating any particular course of action, but by description, careful analysis, the use of reliable knowledge and disciplined thought. This requires an educational system tuned to the realities of national and global trends and consciously designed to prepare successive generations of young men and women for more rational and more compassionate citizenship.

It is all very well to think about what our schools and our society can do; but what about other countries – Russia, for example, or China, India, and all of the developing Third World nations? We must hope that, regardless of ideological and other differences, people elsewhere also will respond to the same compulsions and imperatives of today's world. Our immediate tasks lie within the borders of our own country.

Therefore, as this century draws to a close, we can foresee men and women reviving, redesigning, and updating standards of judgment that have been so badly neglected in our indulgent and overly permissive society – standards to determine the wisdom of future alternatives, to decide what is right and what is wrong, what technology may do and what it must not do. People may then develop a new ethic that recognizes the limits of man's technological power over the non-human environment and over humanity itself.

We can anticipate men and women developing more foresight, recognizing that a decision made today can have consequences into a long future and indeed may be irreversible. People may also become more skilled in thinking about space and understand that something done here in this place could have repercussions around the world.

With this ability to think farther out in time and space, some of the selfishness in human nature might be lessened. The preoccupation of all of us with our own short-sighted concerns might be modified by compassion, by a greater sympathy and understanding for others wherever they may live, by a deeper sense of sharing the earth with people from all other lands and indeed with unborn generations, because they too have a stake in the future.

We can foresee societies where technology is a servant and not the master, where people are more confident that they have control of their own destinies, and where therefore the feelings of alienation, frustration, anger, and lack of power are reduced. We can foresee societies whose citizens place more emphasis, not on their rights, but on their duties, obligations, and responsibilities to others and to society as a whole. In these societies there would be no need to seek security through mass action and the brutality of numbers, through threats of civil disobedience and violence or through excessive dependence on governments.

It would be naive to suggest that people will react in all of these desirable and positive ways. They could react in precisely the opposite and disastrous directions. But the choices are there. What choice will be made, what life will be like beyond the twentieth century, will depend ultimately on human nature. Over fifty years ago, Lord Moulton, an eminent British judge, wrote about an area of human conduct that lies between positive law and absolute freedom. He called it the domain of "Obedience to the Unenforceable" and defined it as covering "all cases of right doing where there is no one to make you do it but yourself . . . a realm that includes the sway of duty, fairness, sympathy, taste, and all the other things that make life beautiful and society possible. . . . Mere obedience to law does not measure the greatness of a nation. Nor is the licence of behaviour, which so often accompanies the absence of law, and which is miscalled liberty, a proof of greatness. The true test is the extent to which individuals can be trusted to obey self-imposed law."

The existence of choices does not, then, leave us with a totally dark picture of the future. Humanity is at a crossroads; as Albert Camus has written, it is "halfway between sunshine and shadow, somewhere between yes and no." Our schools must do their utmost to help young men and women realize that this is a challenging and hopeful position. For these young people the choices lie mainly in the area of obedience to the unenforceable; if their answers turn out to be yes, they will have participated in the creation of a new humanity, the coming of another renaissance.

SELECTED OISE PUBLICATIONS ON CANADA STUDIES

What Culture? What Heritage?
A Study of Civic Education in Canada
A. B. Hodgetts

The author reports on a nation-wide investigation of students' attitudes toward their country, its two founding nations, regional differences of language and culture, and political and social problems. The findings are a severe indictment of what young people of the '60s have learned about their own country.
122 pages, 1968.

DOCUMENTS IN CANADIAN HISTORY
Virginia R. Robeson, general editor

An outgrowth of a project jointly sponsored by the Canada Studies Foundation and the Ontario Institute for Studies in Education
This series offers a valuable resource for the study of the life and times of Canadians in the 18th and 19th centuries. The selections, chosen by a large group of teachers, draw on a rich variety of original sources – debates, early maps, diaries, books, journals, speeches, and newspaper reports and articles. Of interest to students of Canadian history at both intermediate and senior secondary levels, as well as to the general reader.

New France: 1713–1760
Covers colonial policy; administration; the seigneurial régime and agriculture; trade and industry; towns; and daily life.   87 pages, 1977.

Lower Canada in the 1830s
Covers population and migration; land granting and agriculture; commerce, industry, and transportation; politics; and religion, education, and society.
109 pages, 1977.

Upper Canada in the 1830s
Covers similar topics to the above.   111 pages, 1977.

Debates about Canada's Future: 1868–1896
Covers the problems and conflicts centring on Confederation; the question of Canada's role in the British Empire; Canada's North American context; and race, religion, and politics.   116 pages, 1977.

Documents in Canadian History: A Teacher's Guide
Introduces the four books in the series and suggests how each might be used. Also includes a substantial list of titles in French and English for background reading on the periods covered.   33 pages, 1977.

LABOR/MANAGEMENT ISSUES
Robert M. Laxer, general editor

An outgrowth of a project on labor and management relations jointly sponsored by the Canada Studies Foundation and the Ontario Institute for Studies in Education. Suitable for use with secondary school students.

Unions and the Collective Bargaining Process
A basic text on the structure and operation of unions, and their interaction with management. Topics include organizing, negotiations, collective agreements, and grievance procedures, with good illustrative examples. Alternative patterns for resolving labor–management conflict are explored.   77 pages, 1978.

Union Organization and Strikes
Case studies examining four major strikes – Grand Trunk (1919), Ford (1945), Stelco (1946), and Asbestos (1949) – that contributed significantly to establishing union recognition and union security in Canada. In each strike, the attitude of the government and the role it played in the dispute were important factors in determining present-day legislation and the place unions occupy in our society.   103 pages, 1978.

Technological Change and the Work Force
The focus is on Canada's experience of the continuing industrial revolution – the shift from craft to industrial occupations and on to further rapid changes in skill and modern specialization demands. Included is an account of the efforts of organized worker associations to influence the impact of technological innovation upon the nature of working life.   64 pages, 1978.

CANADIAN PUBLIC FIGURES ON TAPE
One-hour taped interviews with ten noted Canadians who have made a major contribution to government. Series includes John Diefenbaker, T. C. Douglas, Walter Gordon, Judy LaMarsh, Maurice Lamontagne, René Lévesque, Paul Martin, Lester Pearson, J. W. Pickersgill, and Joey Smallwood.

CANADIAN GOVERNMENT POLICY AND PROCESS
Eighteen half-hour taped interviews with prominent Canadians about the offices they hold and how they fit into the Canadian political system. Topics include *The Crown* (Roly Michener), *The Judiciary* (Bora Laskin), *The Cabinet* (Donald Jamieson), *The Bureaucracy* (Sylvia Ostry), and many others.

CANADIAN CONTEMPORARY ISSUES ON TAPE
An open-ended series of taped interviews with experts on Canadian foreign policy, past and present, immigration, the economy, and many other issues of national concern.

A catalogue offering further information on these and other OISE publications may be obtained from Publications Sales, 252 Bloor Street West, Toronto, Ontario M5S 1V6.